MEN-AT-ARMS SERIES

EDITOR: MARTIN WINDROW

French Foreign Legion

Text by MARTIN WINDROW

Color plates by MICHAEL ROFFE

HIPPOCRENE
BOOKS, INC.

Hippocrene Books, Inc.
171 Madison Avenue
New York, N.Y. 10016

First published in the United States 1973

ISBN 0 88254 160 9

First published in Great Britain in 1971 by
Osprey Publishing Ltd, P.O. Box 25,
707 Oxford Road, Reading, Berkshire

The preparation of this text would have been
impossible without reference to the following works.
The author gratefully acknowledges his debt to:
The Foreign Legion by Patrick Turnbull (Heinemann,
London); *Mémorial de la Légion Étrangère* (Sélection
de France, Paris); *Et voici la Légion Étrangère*
(Editions André Bonne, Paris); *La Légion Étrangère*
by Georges Blond (Editions Stock, Paris); and in
particular to the most detailed English-language
study of this subject, *The Story of the French Foreign
Legion* by Edgar O'Ballance (Faber, London).
The author is also most grateful for the assistance of
the Service Historique de la Légion and the staff of
Képi Blanc.

The superior numbers in the text refer to the Notes on
page 35.

Printed in Great Britain

Introduction

It is arguable that no body of fighting men in the whole history of European arms has been so inundated with ill-informed publicity as the French Foreign Legion. For more than a century this famous corps has been alternately libelled and romanticized by a steady stream of sentimental fiction, ill-founded horror stories in the popular press, indignant newspaper leaders, and catch-penny film and television scripts. Some of the most

persistent myths are still in wide currency today: that the Legion is a penal unit of thieves and killers expelled from other French regiments; that it is a labour corps; that it is an unreliable mob of drunken thugs; that the discipline is brutal; that it is today composed entirely of ex-Nazi war criminals; even, that it has been disbanded.

This writer hopes that the following brief account of the Legion's history may serve to correct some of the more blatant myths, at the same time as informing those interested in military matters of the appearance of the *légionnaire* down the years. Perhaps the first fact to be put firmly on the record is that the Legion is very much alive today. It is a sophisticated force of motorized infantry, airborne troops and light armour totalling perhaps 15,000 men, whose main combat units are currently based in France, Corsica, Madagascar, Somalia, Tchad and Tahiti. Far from being a penal unit, its standards of physical fitness, military expertise, discipline, equipment, food, pay and welfare are equal to the best in any army in the world. It has given a second chance in life to those who, either by their own weakness or by the political injustices of the last 140 years, have found themselves without homes or allegiance. In return, generations of *légionnaires* have built a tradition of defiance, endurance and self-sufficiency which has won for their corps some of the most highly decorated colours in the French Army, and which has turned a Legion posting into a prize sought after by the best graduates of St Cyr.

An old and crudely retouched photograph of considerable rarity, showing a légionnaire of the Legion's 2e Régiment Étranger in Morocco, probably just before the First World War. Points of interest are the capote with rolled epaulettes, the pack with bivouac poles, the 1886 Lebel rifle, and the unofficial but widely-used neck-cloth buttoned to the pale khaki képi. The V-shaped mark on the képi is the result of bad retouching. (Radio Times Hulton Picture Library)

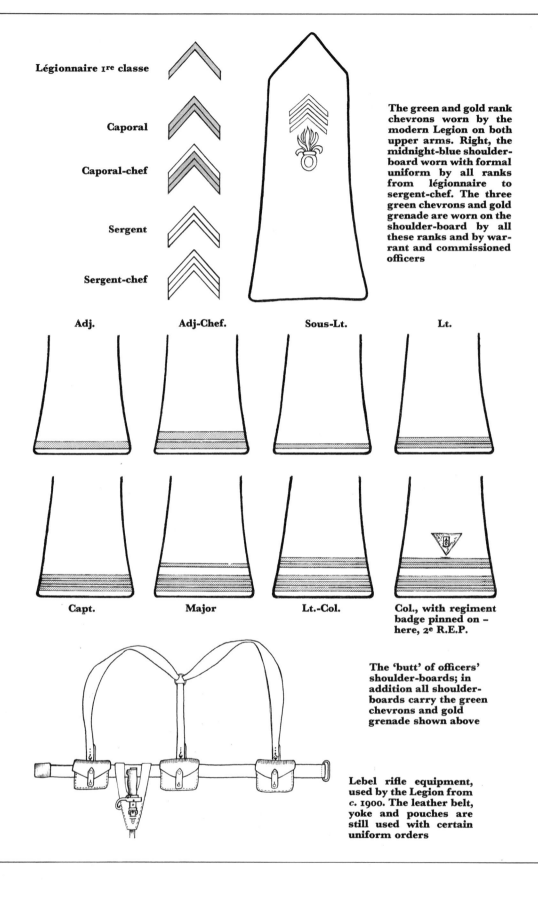

Légionnaire 1re classe

Caporal

Caporal-chef

Sergent

Sergent-chef

The green and gold rank chevrons worn by the modern Legion on both upper arms. Right, the midnight-blue shoulder-board worn with formal uniform by all ranks from légionnaire to sergent-chef. The three green chevrons and gold grenade are worn on the shoulder-board by all these ranks and by warrant and commissioned officers

Adj. Adj-Chef. Sous-Lt. Lt.

Capt. Major Lt.-Col. Col., with regiment badge pinned on – here, 2e R.E.P.

The 'butt' of officers' shoulder-boards; in addition all shoulder-boards carry the green chevrons and gold grenade shown above

Lebel rifle equipment, used by the Legion from c. 1900. The leather belt, yoke and pouches are still used with certain uniform orders

The Old Legion

On 9 March 1831 King Louis-Philippe of France signed a royal ordinance which declared that a legion of foreigners was to be formed for military service outside France, that recruiting was to commence forthwith, and that the title of the formation would be Légion Étrangère. A supplementary ordinance was hastily issued nine days later, declaring that Frenchmen were forbidden to enlist in this force.

The idea, attributed to Marshal Soult, was founded in cynicism. France had recently embarked on an adventure in Algeria which was causing extremely heated political discussion. Several mercenary regiments, notably the Swiss Guards and the Regiment of Hohenlohe, had recently been disbanded, and the streets of Paris were full of discharged soldiers. They begged, brawled, drank, molested passers-by and were generally a threat to law and order. Only eight months on his tottering throne, the King could not afford to have this trouble-hungry pool of malcontents in his capital, ripe for the approaches and manipulations of his enemies. If they could be drafted to Algeria they would be well out of the way, and high casualties and poor conditions would not be as politically explosive among mercenaries as among the husbands, brothers and sons of Frenchwomen. For practical reasons it was decided that each company would be composed of men of common nationality; and in the interests of speed and in contrast to normal practice, no identity papers would be demanded of would-be recruits. This policy of 'no questions asked' was later extended to a guarantee of complete anonymity. (Although this total sanctuary is no longer offered to the recruit, the Legion still blocks all inquiries about a *légionnaire* until they have sought his permission to confirm his presence in the Legion, and the withholding of such permission is considered to close the matter, whatever the nature of the inquiry. No papers are required of a recruit, and he is accepted under any name he chooses.)

One Maj. Sicco, a veteran of the Retreat from Moscow in 1812, was placed in charge of a recruiting centre at Langres, and was soon doing a brisk trade. Ex-soldiers and foreign transients were joined by criminals on the run and gullible would-be colonists who were promised land in Algeria. French local authorities tried to unload their 'undesirable' element on the Legion, thus provoking the second ordinance of 18th March. It proved no barrier then, and still fails to dissuade Frenchmen who wish to join; traditionally, they declare a false name and Swiss or Belgian nationality.

This motley collection of humanity was shipped off to Algeria in several batches during the second half of 1831, and simply unloaded on the quayside. Their presence was a serious embarrassment to the authorities. They had no uniforms, equipment, organization or discipline. There were far too few officers and N.C.O.s, and some had been 'elected' by their own men on dubious claims of previous experience. No arrangements had been made for their reception, and the whole exercise was characterized by indecent haste to get them off the soil of France. Some were too old, others too young; some were chronic drunkards, or crippled, or diseased. The duped 'colonists' among them showed a willingness to take out their rage and frustration on any officer who dared approach them. They were, in a word, a rabble. Their transformation came at the hands of a Swiss colonel named Stoffel.

With patience and ruthlessness Stoffel and his staff (largely composed of officers and N.C.O.s bribed to serve a term in this riff-raff by offers of extra pay) sorted the misfits from the potential soldiers, and wrought a semblance of order. The national companies were formed into battalions[1] as follows, although the full picture was not to emerge for about two years:

1st Battalion: former Swiss Guards and Hohenlohe Regiment
2nd Battalion: Swiss and Germans
3rd Battalion: Swiss and Germans
4th Battalion: Spanish
5th Battalion: Italians and Sardinians
6th Battalion: Belgians and Dutch
7th Battalion Poles (each battalion had an extra Polish company)

In time the bulk of the force settled in camps

Algeria and Morocco, the cradle of the Legion. Note that the international frontiers illustrated are the modern ones

around Algiers, the 4th Battalion marching off to Oran and the 6th to Bône. The reputation of the Legion spread alarmingly, and they were soon known as a murderous crowd of thieving sots who would beat up officers as soon as look at them. Many voices called for the abandonment of the whole exercise, but for some reason – probably apathy – the Legion remained on the rolls, and the recruits came in at a steady rate. The strength, initially 3,000, rose to 5,000 and stabilized at that point. Patient training, undeniably harsh discipline and back-breaking construction work sweated the mischief out of most of them, but there were frequent vicious fights due to the idiotic segregation of nationalities. The feuds and hatreds of a dozen countries flared up again in the Legion.

In Algeria at this period a population of wild tribesmen owed allegiance to nobody and warred constantly. The centres of population were held by force by a succession of beys owing nominal allegiance to Constantinople, and keeping their thrones only through the efforts of units of nominally Turkish janissaries. These beys were more often than not European or Arab adventurers. By the mid-1830s, after the escalation of a series of petty slights, some 35,000 French troops held down a thin coastal corridor, along the fringes of which the native population raided and

burned with enthusiasm. Paris could not make up its mind to admit its colonial hunger and press on with open occupation of the whole area. This led to a frustrating and dangerous series of vacillations in policy which cost lives and time.

The Legion first saw action as a result of its construction work on a belt of blockhouses to consolidate the French perimeter. On 27 April 1832 some companies of Swiss and Germans from the 3rd Battalion were sent to eject a group of Arabs who had occupied a building known as Maison Carrée and were harassing labour gangs in the area. The buildings were taken in a sharp skirmish, a counter-attack was held off, and the Legion retained Maison Carrée as an outpost. Other minor attacks were repulsed, but in May a Legion officer and 26 men were caught in the open nearby and wiped out by Arab horsemen – who left more than 70 dead on the field.

1832 saw the arrival on the scene of Abdul-el-Kader, an Arab leader of great tenacity and skill. The son of a marabout or holy man, he was young, determined and brave, and attracted an enthusiastic following. In May and November he made two unsuccessful advances on Oran, and the Spanish 4th Battalion of the Legion was involved in the second of these battles, at Sidi Chabal. Meanwhile the Italians of the 5th Battalion were

REGIMENTAL BADGES

(Left to right)
Regimental badge of the 1er Régiment Étranger, bearing the traditional Mexican eagle motif

The 1er R.E.C., formed in the 1920s largely from White Russian refugees, and now an armoured unit equipped with AMX-13 tanks

The 2e R.E.C., disbanded in the mid-1960s. The design led to the regimental nickname of 'Dauphin Étranger'

Roman remains in the Near East inspired the badge of the 6e R.E.I. stationed in Syria for many years, and disbanded after fighting for the Vichy Government against Free French forces

(R.G. Windrow collection)

fighting a series of small actions around Bône. In June 1832 Col. Stoffel departed; to this able officer must go much of the credit for turning the rabble who had been dumped on the Algiers quayside into a fighting unit in only twelve months. His successor, Col. Combe, who brought with him the first regimental colour, was soon replaced in his turn by the energetic Col. Bernelle.

During 1833 the Italian and Spanish *légionnaires* saw action on several occasions, the latter winning particular praise for their expertise in broken country guerrilla-type operations, in contrast to the basically European-style set-piece tactics pursued with questionable success by more conventional units. Notable among these actions were clashes at Arzew and Mostagenem. 1834 was less eventful, as the French were trying to turn Kader into a client ruler by recognizing him as Emir of Mascara, and the Governor-General favoured a policy of consolidation. Kader bided his time and established his authority over various local leaders while building up his strength with the aid of European adventurers. In 1835 he felt strong

enough to make another attempt to eject the French, and advanced on Tlemcen. He by-passed the town, and ran up against the hastily assembled French punitive column at a pass in the foothills called Moulay Ishmael on 26th June.

Companies of Spanish, Italian and Polish *légionnaires* were included in the column, three companies of the latter forming the advance guard which ran into Kader's forces in the pass. Unable to force a passage, they were soon hard put to it to prevent the Arabs flooding through and driving in the head of the column. While the cumbersome wagons which accompanied the column were being turned round, more Arabs appeared on the flanks, but were held off by a screen of Italian *légionnaires*. While these companies guarded the flanks at heavy cost, the Poles stood firm in the pass, and formed the rearguard when the retreat was sounded and the painful withdrawal to the plain commenced. After disengaging and spending a day licking their wounds the French began to return to Oran. They were harried constantly, and the Legion bore the worst of the fighting in exposed positions. On the Macta salt-marsh the column ran into a serious ambush, in the course of which Arabs reached the wagons and killed the wounded. That the column managed to join up again and limp into Oran under cover of night was largely due to the efforts of the *légionnaires*.

The twin disasters of Moulay Ishmael and Macta caused severe damage to French morale, while that of the Arabs soared. Nevertheless it was officially noticed that the 'thieves, drunkards and vagabonds' of the Legion had fought superbly. Before this new assessment of its worth could become widely known, however, a shabby political manœuvre occurred which killed off more *légionnaires* than Kader had done.

Spain and the Carlist War, 1835-8

When civil war broke out in Spain late in 1834, France honoured a commitment to aid the 'Christino' supporters of the Spanish Queen Regent by ceding the Legion lock, stock and barrel. This cheap way out of an obligation was politically attractive, as it involved no 'official' French soldiers, but morally disgraceful. Legion officers protested in vain, and over half elected to share the fortunes of their men.

Under Bernelle's command the Legion landed at Tarragona in August 1835. The national battalions were split up (although national companies were retained) and scattered units saw action in Catalonia for some months. A Carlist victory at Estella was followed by a Christino winter advance, during which the Legion suffered severe hardship around Pamplona. In 1836 Legion victories were won at Tirapegui and Zubiri, but at the end of the year Bernelle was replaced; his protests at the poor support his command was receiving had annoyed Paris. Col. Conrad took over in November, and found that the original strength of 5,000 men had been reduced by starvation, disease and desertion to three small battalions. Neither France nor Spain wished the responsibility of supplying the Legion, and while

they wrangled the men starved and froze, lacking the most basic necessities of equipment.

In March 1837 the Legion moved into Aragon, and on 2nd June was virtually wiped out in a savage fight with Carlist mercenary forces at Barbastro. Neither side gave quarter, and Conrad became the first of many Legion colonels to die at the head of his men. The survivors, who were all that remained of the heroes of Moulay Ishmael, were simply left to rot at Pamplona. Despite the pleas of their officers, who showed great devotion to their men, no support or relief was forthcoming. When the unit was officially disbanded on 6 December 1838 only about 500 men remained; 23 officers and more than 3,600 men had died in the campaign. It is impressive to find that nearly 400 of the survivors elected to return to Algeria to join the New Legion.

Algeria, 1837-54

A royal ordinance of December 1835 had created a second French Foreign Legion; recruits were shipped to Spain initially, but were later retained in France and given basic training. At the turn of 1836–7 a force of 800 under Maj. Bedeau took ship to Algeria. By July 1837 a regimental establishment was possible, and in October the two battalions took part in the assault on Constantine. Since the defeats of June 1835 the Arabs had been very active, and the main area of operations had been in the east, on the fringes of the Kabylie Mountains. The Bey of Constantine had been a leading figure in the unrest, especially after an unsuccessful attempt on his city in 1836.

The October assault was mounted by strong forces from Bône, and on 13th October, after artillery preparation, three columns in which Legion units were prominent, successfully stormed Constantine. In the months that followed half the 'eastern' battalion of the Legion was stationed at Constantine and half at Bône, while the 1st Battalion remained at Algiers. By late in 1839 recruiting had reached such a point that four battalions were on the establishment, totalling some 3,500 men, and a better type of officer was being attracted to the Legion.

Kader soon went on the offensive again, having built an army of 6,000, including 150 trained gunners. 1840 saw a French advance on Medea in which the Legion's 1st and 4th Battalions were prominent, smashing an Arab blocking position in the pass of Tenia de Mouzaia on both the outward and return marches. More fighting in this pass occurred in June when the same units marched on Meliana. The Legion provided a garrison near Meliana after the town had been captured and the main force withdrawn. This was promptly besieged and only 288 men out of two battalions remained alive by the time the relief force arrived in October. The same units were later decimated by disease at Fondouk. The 3rd Battalion saw sharp action at Djidjelli while operating out of Bône.

A firm policy of occupation characterized 1840–2, and Gen. Bugeard's energetic tactics – based on flying columns with mule-borne artillery rather than on massive static positions – drove Kader to take refuge in Morocco. The Legion took to these operations gladly, and earned a blood-chilling reputation among the Arabs for appearing without warning and fighting like devils. 1841 saw a reorganization into two regiments, the 1er Régiment Étranger (under the able Col. Mauret from 1843 onwards) operating in the west, and the 2e R.E. in the east around Bône and Setif, the latter eventually becoming its base. In 1843 another rising inspired by Kader was quickly cut to pieces by the French flying columns, and Kader retreated to Morocco once more. In this year, in the course of establishing a series of supply depots – 'Biscuit-villes' – for the columns, the 3rd Battalion first planted the Legion's flag at Sidi-bel-Abbes, about 60 miles south of Oran. Attacks on the camp in 1844 led to the first permanent buildings; and by the time the Legion left Algeria in the 1960s Sidi-bel-Abbes had become a garrison town entirely built by légionnaire labour, and the spiritual home of the Legion, housing its museum and archives.

Kader's periodic retreats into Morocco led to Bugeard's occupation of the Moroccan town of Oujda in 1844. He was only restrained from marching on the capital, Fez, by frantic cables from Paris. His subsequent retreat was interpreted

A fine print by Benigni showing an N.C.O. in full campaign kit of the 1850s, with the central cartridge pouch from which the nickname 'leatherbellies' was derived

as weakness, and the Sultan led a 16,000-man army to the Algerian border. On 13th August, after a forced march with nearly 8,000 troops including the entire 1er R.E., Bugeard defeated the Moroccans in a night attack which led to several hours of fighting. The Sultan was forced to sign a pact agreeing to French rights of pursuit across his borders, a right which was vigorously exercised. Kader's subsequent forays became more hazardous, but he appeared to lead a charmed life, and was regarded with grudging affection by the légionnaires, as their own personal enemy. He was eventually captured and exiled in December 1847, and relative peace descended on western Algeria.

In the east the Bey of Constantine – driven from his mountain fortress but still active – was constantly fomenting trouble among the Kabylie tribes. There followed years of fighting, with vain French attempts to penetrate the rebels' sanctuary in the grim Kabylie highlands. In February 1844 the future Marshal McMahon commanded a

Légionnaires photographed in the late nineteenth century (possibly on the occasion of the half-centenary in 1881) wearing various uniforms of the Legion between the 1840s and 1880s. (Radio Times Hulton Picture Library)

bataillon de marche[2] composed of the *compagnies d'élite*[3] of the 2e R.E. which did well at Biskra and M'Chounech. M'Chounech, a ridge position held by 3,000 tribesmen who had repulsed two attacks by two French line battalions, fell to the single Legion battalion in twenty minutes. The same, officer led the same unit in other battles in 1851, and in 1853 both regiments were on campaign; the Beni Snassen tribe rose in the west, attracting the attentions of the 1er R.E.

The Crimea, 1854-6

In June 1854 each regiment was ordered to provide three battalions for the campaign against Russia, and the garrisons of Sidi-bel-Abbes and Setif were accordingly stripped. This Brigade Étrangère was among the units which landed briefly at Varna in Bulgaria, where it was rocked by a cholera epidemic which carried off both regimental commanders and 200 *légionnaires*. On arriving in the Crimea the brigade was split; a *bataillon de marche* composed of all the *compagnies d'élite* was posted to Canrobert's division, and the balance were intended for second-line duties.

The *bataillon de marche* did very well at the storming of the heights of Alma on 20 September 1854. They impressed Canrobert with their indifference to enemy fire, an indifference which cost them 5 officers and 55 men dead and wounded. The Legion also fought at Inkerman in small numbers. Canrobert decided he could not waste such troops on line-of-communication duties, and brought up the rest of the brigade. The whole contingent fought in the hellish trench warfare around Sebastopol in the winter of 1854-5, and fought in several actions when the Allies took the initiative again in the spring. Notable was a night attack on 1 May 1855 in which Col. Vienot (after whom the Legion's Aubagne depot is named) became the second Legion colonel to die at the head of his men. In another push on 7th June the Legion captured a series of positions known as the White Works, and *légionnaires* played their part in the sapping and raiding which culminated in the major assaults of 8th September. The Brigade Étrangère was fully committed, and groups of volunteers also formed scaling-ladder parties who advanced in front of other French units. On 10th September in the streets of Sebastopol Gen. Bazaine – once a Legion sergeant – was given command.

The horrors of winter trench warfare – which had cost the Legion 72 officers and more than 1,600 men dead and wounded or disabled by disease and cold – were apparently offset soon afterwards by a period of patrolling and foraging in open country. During this time the *légionnaires* seem to have acquired a widespread reputation for 'liberating' fresh vegetables for the pot. They added the nickname 'The Cabbage Brigade' to the one they already had – 'The Leatherbellies', a reference to the large leather cartridge pouch worn on the centre of the belt at the front.

No major actions ensued before the brigade returned to Algeria. They received Crimean Service Medals for this campaign; and their spell in Europe brought one colourful figure to the fore. One Mina, a Spanish ex-bandit of chequered past, was serving under the name of Martinez, and now rose to the rank of major for his conduct in the Crimea.

The Reduction of Kabylia

During 1854 the Arabs took advantage of the Legion's weakness (only two battalions remained in Algeria) to cause havoc. When the troops returned from the Crimea larger-scale French operations became possible, but central Kabylia still defied all attempts at pacification. 1856 saw

A French ambulance column in the Crimea, pictured in the 'Illustrated London News'. (Radio Times Hulton Picture Library)

the fifteenth unsuccessful French attempt to penetrate this area in force since 1838.

A widespread reorganization of the Legion took place in this year, with the arrival in Algeria of a regiment of Swiss mercenaries formed by Napoleon III under the command of his friend Col. Ochenbein. Not ready in time for the Crimea, the Swiss regiment was eventually shipped to Africa and – by virtue of Ochenbein's seniority and influence – became the new 1er R.E. The veterans of the Brigade Étrangère were formed into a 2e R.E. Both units took part in the great final assault on Kabylia in the early summer of 1857, when four divisions approached the central plateaux from four different directions, with a total strength of 35,000 men. Two battalions from the 2e R.E., providing the advance guard for the column moving eastwards, fought a major action on 24th June at Ischeriden. Once more under the eye of their old commander, Gen. McMahon, the *légionnaires* took a key position which had repulsed two regiments of line infantry – and took it with the bayonet, without firing a single shot, within thirty minutes of receiving the order to advance. Ischeriden was the key, and three weeks of mopping up saw the area nominally pacified at last. The 1er R.E. marched back to Setif and the 2e R.E. to Sidi-bel-Abbes, for a spell of road-building and police work, but not before a speech of gratitude from McMahon and the presentation of a new colour. More valuable still was the *légionnaires'* growing reputation among the tribes, who had a healthy respect for the 'blue-backed beetles', as they called them, in reference to the buttoned-back greatcoats.

Italy, 1859

Both Legion regiments took part in the brief war of 1859 between Victor Emmanuel of Sardinia and his French allies, and the Austrians. On 11th May both regiments came under the command of Gen. Espinasse at Genoa, as part of McMahon's 2nd Corps. On 4th June, drawn up on the extreme left of the French line, the *légionnaires* advanced on Magenta. The approaches to this important rail centre were wooded and cultivated, and guarded by Austrian outposts; one of these, at Marcollo, cost the Legion heavy losses including Col. Chabrière, who fell at the head of the 2e R.E. The regiment was rallied by Maj. Martinez, of Crimean fame, and swept on into the outskirts of the town. The 2nd Corps played a leading part in this French victory; Legion casualties were in excess of 250. The under-strength 1er R.E. remained in Milan to recruit while the 2e R.E. took part in the two-week pursuit of the Austrians which led to the victory of Solferino; the regiment was now led by Col. Martinez.

Despite the kudos won at Magenta and Solferino, the Legion was subjected to a period of neglect after its return to Algeria. There was no campaigning to do, and as always in peace-time, morale suffered. In 1861 the 1er R.E. at Philippeville was so reduced in strength that it was disbanded, and the few remaining companies joined the other regiment at Sidi-bel-Abbes, the whole simply being known as the Régiment Étranger, with a strength of some 2,500 under the command of Col. Butet. After two depressing years the Legion's junior officers sent a petition direct to the Emperor requesting a posting to a foreign war which had since broken out. This insolent but spirited move scandalized the generals but had its dubious reward; in March 1863 Col. Jeanningros led two Legion battalions ashore at Veracruz.

Mexico, 1863-7

French intervention in Mexico dated from 1862, and when their client-ruler Maximilian landed in May 1864 he found that his writ extended no wider than a corridor between Mexico City and Veracruz, maintained with some difficulty by 40,000 troops, many of them French. But by 1864 the Legion's greatest battle honour had been won.

Initially the Legion was employed on patrol, convoy and blockhouse duty in the fever-ridden lowlands of the eastern corridor. A month after their arrival the Legion's 3rd Company, 1st Battalion, was required to provide escort for a bullion convoy. As all officers in this unit were prostrate with fever, three volunteers came forward. These were the battalion adjutant, Capt. Danjou, a veteran of Algeria, the Crimea and Italy who had left a hand at Magenta; Lt. Vilain, the paymaster; and 2nd Lt. Maudet. Both the latter were experienced officers who had come up through the ranks after enlisting illegally, for they were French citizens; and both had been commissioned for gallantry at Magenta.

Before dawn on 30 April 1863 Danjou set out with his two officers and sixty-two *légionnaires*. They marched some considerable distance ahead of the convoy. At first light they halted briefly at a Legion outpost, whose commander offered the under-strength escort an extra platoon, but Danjou refused to strip the small garrison of firepower at a time of incessant guerrilla attacks. At about 7.00 a.m. the escort halted for coffee and bread about a mile beyond a derelict settlement named Camerone. Minutes later the sentries sighted horsemen approaching; these were 800 irregular cavalry led by a local officer of revolutionary troops, Col. Milan, who had ridden ahead of his main force of 1,200 infantry after being warned of the convoy's approach by an informer. The cavalry were well trained and armed with repeating rifles; the Legion at this time carried single-shot Minié weapons.

Danjou formed the habitual hollow square and fell back on Camerone, holding off the cavalry with volley fire; nevertheless, sixteen men and both the supply mules were cut off and captured before the ruins came in sight. They consisted of a two-storey farmhouse, in poor repair but structurally sound, surrounded by a group of outhouses and lean-to sheds grouped around a courtyard, the whole surrounded by an adobe wall. But Mexican snipers were already in possession of the upper storey, and it was under incessant fire that the little group of *légionnaires* set up a makeshift perimeter in the lower storey, the sheds and around the wall. They fought off several rushes by the dismounted cavalry, but suffered a steady trickle of casualties from the crossfire. By 9.00 a.m. the sun was up, the wounded lay beyond help in the courtyard under the rifles of the snipers, and the Mexicans had drawn closer. A surrender demand was rejected, and Danjou made each man swear not to surrender – some say, on his wooden hand. He was killed by a sniper in the farmhouse at about 11.00 a.m.

Vilain took command, and the 3rd Company held off numerous attacks by the cavalry and the 1,200 infantry who had now arrived on the scene. Thirst and sunstroke added to the torment of the increasingly restricted defenders. Vilain lived until about 2.00 p.m. When he fell Maudet took over, seizing a dead man's rifle and rallying the defence to the threatened points. Mexican attempts to fire the buildings added choking smoke to the *légionnaires'* miseries, and the snipers now overlooked the whole area held by the French. Time and again charges were driven off at point-blank range by disciplined fire from the dwindling band of defenders.

By 5.00 p.m. Maudet had only twelve men left on their feet. He had rejected further surrender demands with choice barrack-room replies, but a massive rush had driven the survivors right out of the farmhouse, restricting them to a few of the out-houses. By 6.00 p.m. he had five men left, and only a handful of ammunition. Knowing that the approaching darkness would bring inevitable defeat, he ordered his five to use their last few rounds. Then they fixed bayonets, pulled aside a barricade, and charged straight across the courtyard at the front ranks of some 1,700 surviving Mexicans.

Milan saw this incredible display of defiance, and managed to save the lives of three of the six – Maine, Berg and Wensel. The others died of their wounds. In all 23 were taken alive from the ruins, of whom 16 survived their short captivity. A single living *légionnaire* was found under the dead, with eight bullet wounds, by Jeanningros and the relief force which arrived on 1st May, alerted by the convoy which had retreated safely on hearing the gunfire. The wooden hand of Capt. Danjou was also found and taken away, to become a sacred relic. Mexican casualties amounted to some 300 dead and at least as many wounded. The Legion prisoners were well treated and exchanged a month later.

The hopeless defence of Camerone became the Legion's most highly regarded battle honour, not for its military significance but for the spirit it showed. The hand of Danjou is the Legion's most revered relic, and is paraded each 30th April

Mexico. At the derelict settlement of Camerone the Legion won its proudest battle honour on 30 April 1863

A clash between chasseurs and Mexican territorials at Los Llanos on 12 February 1863. (Radio Times Hulton Picture Library)

before the 1st Regiment of the Legion at the base depot. The account of the battle is read to every Legion unit on Camerone Day; this is never omitted, and was shouted from fox-hole to fox-hole at Dien Bien Phu weeks before the fall of the fortress. The ashes of the Camerone dead are preserved in a reliquary carved as the Mexican eagle, and are held in rotation in the chapel of each Legion regiment. Every recruit has it drummed into him over and over again during his training that he is personally expected to live up to the standard of uncompromising defiance set by Danjou and his men on 30 April 1863: the Legion must never, ever surrender, and when all hope and means of resistance is gone the *légionnaire* is expected to die weapon in hand, running, walking or crawling towards the enemy.

The Legion stayed in Mexico until February 1867. Its record was unhappy, and included a disastrous defeat at Parras which cost 112 dead. The majority of the campaign was spent in wearying anti-guerilla fighting; the names of Huichapam and Perral stand out in a series of clashes. By March 1867 the Legion was back at Sidi-bel-Abbes; it left 31 officers and 1,917 *légionnaires* on Mexican soil.

France and Algeria, 1867-82

The years 1867–75 were unhappy for the officers and men of the Régiment Étranger. Minor tax-gathering sorties alternated with road-building and deathly monotonous garrison duty in tiny posts in the Sahara. It was in conditions such as these that the abuses sprang up of which novelists have made so much. The officer calibre deterio-rated; in peacetime there was nothing to lure ambitious and dedicated men to the corps, and a succession of disinterested commanders did great damage. Senior N.C.O.s acquired too much un-supervised power, the men went mad with *le cafard*, savage field punishments were – occasion-ally – inflicted; it was an unhappy picture. Let it be noted, however, that never in its history did the Legion resort to flogging. Another argument against easy belief of the traditional horror stories

is the fact that throughout its life the Legion has ensured that stripes are hard to get and almost impossible to keep. Senior warrant officers could be, and are, reduced to the ranks for quite minor offences, a system which obviously protects the men to some extent. The fate of a sadistic N.C.O. suddenly returned to the barrack-room would have been quick in coming and final in effect.

When Napoleon III declared war on Prussia in July 1870 there were many foreigners in France eager to fight; and in her husband's absence the Empress issued a decree establishing a 5th Battalion of the R.E. in Paris. With no genuine connection with the Legion in Algeria, this 5th Battalion was commanded by a Portuguese, Maj. Aragao; it was soon in action and did well at Bel-Air-Les-Aides near Orleans. On 10th October it got bottled up in Bannier, and suffered heavy losses in the subsequent break-out. When it had re-formed it was joined by two *bataillons de marche* from Algeria. The whole force took part in several actions during the French retreat, notably at Cercottes and Chevilly, but despite incidents of true Legion heroism their impact on the situation was naturally small. The *légionnaires* saw combat at Besançon in January 1871, but this was their last battle of the war. All three battalions were used in the vicious street-fighting which crushed the Paris Communes in 1871, and in June they were shipped back to Algeria, where the depleted 5th Battalion was disbanded in December.

Predictably, the French defeat at the hands of the Prussians had repercussions in North Africa, and as 1870 had also been a year of cholera and famine the situation was explosive. A son of Abdul-el-Kader appeared and led an uprising in north-western Algeria, the Ouled Sidi Cheikh tribe burst into flame along the southern borders of Oran Province, and Kabylia was torn by revolt. Until the troops returned from France the predicament of the garrisons was serious; but when the forces were able to build up their strength again they coped with the situation, and by January 1872 all was once more uneasy peace. The Legion had taken part in the Oran Province operations against the Ouled Sidi Cheikh, old enemies of theirs.

A period of intense colonization now began in Algeria. In 1871 Col. de Mallaret began a ten-year term as commander of the Legion, and under this steadying influence many abuses disappeared. In 1875 the name Légion Étrangère was officially fixed; this had, of course, been the original name of the corps, but had fallen into disuse during periods when strength fell to a single regiment.[4] The distinction was largely academic; before and since 1875 there have been periods when the word *légion* was not officially applied, but the *légionnaires* have blithely continued to refer to themselves as the Legion, whatever the ruling of a far-away office in the Army Ministry!

In 1881, during a period of unrest and constant pin-pricks, command passed to Col. Negrier, to whom the Legion owes much. An able and enthusiastic officer who formed a great affection for his hard-bitten charges, he saved them from deterioration into a labour corps and instituted many reforms to ease the lot of the common soldier. On the tactical side he founded the very successful mounted companies. These were equipped with one mule to every two men; one marched while the other rode, and the packs of both were slung on the mule. In this way each man enjoyed periodic rests, and great distances could be covered – over 30 miles a day over the roughest terrain.

Nobody was surprised when the flames of rebellion broke out again in 1882, and the Ouled Sidi Cheikh were predictably in the thick of it. The Legion was active in the area of Geryville, and it was in this region that the great Battle of Chott Tigri was fought in April. This was a desolate valley through which a large French force passed early on the morning of 26th April; two rifle companies and the Mounted Company of the R.E. were escorting a survey party which had been mapping along the Moroccan border west of Geryville. As the 300-odd *légionnaires* and their charges entered the valley a sandstorm blew up, and the column became somewhat scattered. Suddenly, from both sides, a huge force of Arabs materialized and bore down on the French; their total number is believed to have been about 1,800 horsemen and nearly 6,000 on foot.

As always when caught in open country, the *légionnaires* formed square, but since the column had become disjointed three separate groups formed. The Mounted Company was on its own, and about 500 yards behind it were the two

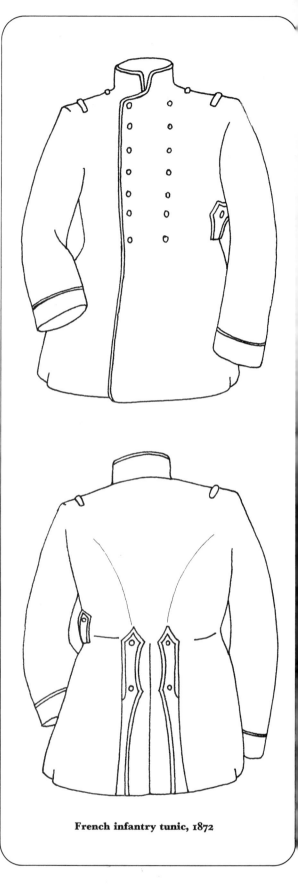

French infantry tunic, 1872

16

infantry companies and the surveying team. Some hundreds of yards behind this square was a small detachment of Legion riflemen, a group of Arab *goumiers* (armed native guides) and some *chasseurs* who were accompanying the column.

The Arab horsemen mounted several charges, all of which were repulsed by disciplined fire, but the warriors on foot moved closer under cover of each charge. When the sandstorm died down the main square managed to move to a slight hillock, and the rearguard fought its way to this and joined up, although some men were cut off in the process. A quarter of a mile away the Mounted Company fought on alone, behind a parapet of dead mules, and under the command of an old *légionnaire* as both officers had been killed early in the action. Hundreds of Arabs swarmed between the two squares, and any further linking up was impossible. Both were under incessant attack, and

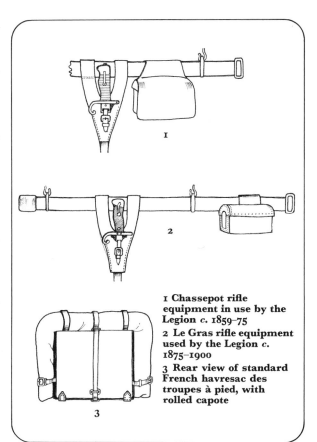

1 Chassepot rifle equipment in use by the Legion c. 1859–75
2 Le Gras rifle equipment used by the Legion c. 1875–1900
3 Rear view of standard French havresac des troupes à pied, with rolled capote

it came to hand-to-hand fighting on several occasions.

The attacks persisted for seven hours before the Arabs began to lose heart. A horrible feature of this action was the fate of those stragglers who had been cut off; they were tortured to death by the Arabs just out of rifle range of their comrades, several of whom died in vain sorties to rescue them. Arab losses must have run into hundreds, but all were carried from the field when the enemy eventually drew off. The Mounted Company at last managed to join up with the main force, and one large square was formed with the wounded in the centre; and late in the afternoon, maintaining this formation and halting frequently to beat off attacks by bands of horsemen, the column struggled painfully out of the valley. At nightfall Col. Negrier met them with a relief column. The Legion lost in this battle 2 officers and 40 *légion-aires* dead, and 3 officers and 28 *légionnaires* wounded. One officer survived with nine bullet wounds and seven sword-cuts. At least three men were killed trying to recover the obviously dead

General Negrier, who commanded the Legion in the early 1880s, was largely responsible for the renewal of morale after a bad period. He took an intense pride in his command and curbed many abuses. (Radio Times Hulton Picture Library)

body of another officer which lay outside the square, to prevent its mutilation by the enemy. This effectively disposes of the myth that Legion officers held authority by fear and brutality; the history of the corps is studded with records of heroism by *légionnaires* attempting to save their officers, or to recover their dead.

This was the last major action fought by *légionnaires* for some years, as the revolts died down and the usual wary peace settled over Oran Province. The Legion did much building and road-laying, and the Mounted Company was frequently out on column policing the area. The number of battalions in Algeria rose to six, and the Legion was once again split into two regiments of three battalions in 1885.

Indo-China, 1883-95

In September 1883 Negrier left the Legion to command one of the French contingents being sent to Indo-China, where France had been extending her influence since about the middle of the century. So deep had his respect for his black sheep become that he agitated for a force of *légionnaires* to be included in his command. The 1st Battalion was shipped to Haiphong in November, and moved up to Hanoi where a force was assembling for an assault on the forts of Son Tay and Bac Ninh.

An army of 25,000 Chinese irregulars – 'Black Flags' – had been sent down from Yunnan to eject the French from Tonkin; they were little more than marauder bands under local war-lords, but they were formidable jungle fighters on ground of their own choosing. They had a fair proportion of modern arms and some old cannon, and although weak in co-ordination for major operations they were past-masters of ambush and infiltration. Their brick fort at Son Tay was screened by stockades, and was situated about 30 miles from Hanoi on the Claire River. The French sent an admiral to command the assault, with a force of 5,000 marines (*marsouins*, or colonial infantry), regular line troops and *légionnaires*. The attack went in on 16 December

1883, and the Legion was first through the stockades and the gates. A Legion sergeant leapt over the secondary defences carrying the colour. The *légionnaires* followed and after a stiff hour of bayonet work the French were in possession of the fort.

A second Legion battalion arrived to join Negrier early in 1884, and both units took part in the capture of Bac Ninh in March. After this the battalions parted, the 1st operating around Tuyen Quang and the 2nd around Hung-Hoa. Both became adept at jungle techniques, almost invariably taking the point when in column, and frequently ambushing would-be ambushers. Exhausting patrol work along the river banks and in the swamps took a heavy toll, both from wounds and disease.

A major battle was fought at Tuyen Quang in January and February 1885. After its capture this old fort was garrisoned by the 1st and 2nd Companies of the Legion's 1st Battalion and two companies of a regular regiment, totalling 390 men. Between August 1884 and early 1885 the Black Flags infiltrated the area steadily, but as the garrison was well provisioned the High Command did not react immediately. By January some 20,000 Chinese had surrounded the fort, and on 26th January a fierce assault was repulsed with difficulty. A series of mine explosions, sapping advances and mass attacks alternated for more than a month. By the time Negrier's relief column make contact with the southern elements of the besiegers at Hoa Moc on 2nd March, the garrison was in desperate straits but still defiant. More than 50 yards of the wall had been blown down, and incessant attacks had only been held by hand-to-hand fighting in the breaches.

By early 1885 the 3rd and 4th Battalions of the Legion had landed in South-East Asia, the latter seeing service on Formosa. Sporadic fighting continued for ten years, but no pitched battles of any size were fought, the Black Flags preferring the classic guerrilla tactics at which they excelled. The last significant clash took place in 1895. The Legion battalions, grouped together as the Régiment de Marche d'Afrique au Tonkin, settled down to garrison duty and police action which lasted, relatively undisturbed, until 1941.

Dahomey and the Sudan, 1892

A small but dramatic campaign was fought in the summer and autumn of 1892 by a *bataillon de marche* of the Legion led by Col. Faurex. This unit was included in Col. Dodd's force, which landed in August 1892 at Cotonou in Dahomey, the small African kingdom between modern Togo and Nigeria. Excuses for the landing were provided by broken treaties and the harassment of French trading posts in the interior as well as by the revolting practices of the Dahomeyan monarchy, which was founded on slave traffic and massive festivals of human sacrifice. King Behazin's capital of Abomey was guarded by 150 miles of thick jungle and fever-ridden swamp. His 10,000 warriors were not very formidable foes, although a picked regiment of 'Amazons' – warrior maidens who displayed great spirit, and had the best of the assorted firearms at the King's disposal – was a force to be reckoned with.

The Legion battalion, drawn from the two regiments in Algeria, frequently provided the advance guard for the column, which moved up-country late in August. Each night the force formed square; and even so it was nearly overrun

on 18th September by a dawn attack. In leading a bayonet charge to clear the square after a break-through by 'Amazons' and male warriors, Faurex was killed. Some 800 Africans were killed in this clash at Dogba. Further delaying actions were fought by the Dahomeyan army on 4th October at Porguessa, and at Koto on 14th October. The last battle took place at Kana, within sight of the

A Mahut print of a soldier of the Legion in Dahomey in 1892; it was in this campaign that the légionnaires came up against King Behazin's formidable regiment of female warriors

skull-bedecked huts of the King. The Legion was prominent in all these actions.

In September 1892 Col. Archinard, the officer entrusted with pacifying French western and central Africa in the path of the projected trans-continental railway, requested a company of the Legion for use in hunting down troublesome slavers. Volunteers were picked for their youth and fitness, and the unit operated for about a year, as a mule-mounted company. Several actions were fought, and the *légionnaires* are calculated to have covered some 12,000 miles in Guinea, Senegal, Volta and the Sudan. Their success was such that their sudden withdrawal is inexplicable.

Dahomey. In 1892 a bataillon de marche of the Legion landed at Cotonou and marched through Dogba to Abomey

Madagascar, 1895

A *bataillon de marche* of *légionnaires* served with Gen. Metzinger's brigade in the invasion of Madagascar in 1895. Ostensibly to aid the Sakalava tribe against the dominant Hovas, the French landed in April of that year, at Majunga on the west coast. The capital of Tananarive was in the central mountains, and the best roads (and thus the Hovas' main defences) lay between the east coast and the central plateau. In choosing to advance from the 'back door' the French command laid themselves open to appalling difficulties; the tracks were hopelessly inadequate, the climate lethal to Europeans, and the diseases of the region rampant.

The Legion played an important part in the advance, which did not reach Tananarive until mid-September. It was found that their casualties from disease were much fewer than those of other units, thought to be due to superior sanitary discipline and the fact that the *légionnaires* did not mix freely with the other troops. The result was that the Legion was more often than not at the point of the column, and bore more than its share of fighting and road-building. Actions were fought at Naked Heights, Suburbieville, Andriba and Tsinaindry; all these positions were cleared successfully, usually by Legion advance guards, at bayonet-point. In the whole campaign only 7 French soldiers died as a result of combat, of whom 5 were *légionnaires*; but in the Legion battalion alone, 226 died of disease and heatstroke[5]. The Legion was subsequently employed in putting down rebellion on the island.

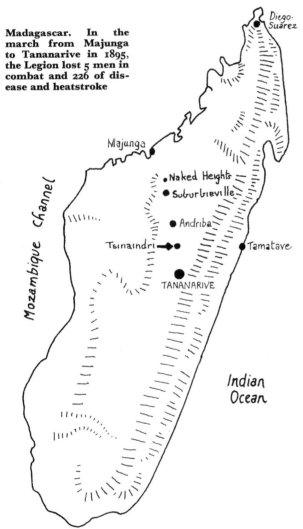

Madagascar. In the march from Majunga to Tananarive in 1895, the Legion lost 5 men in combat and 226 of disease and heatstroke

North Africa, 1890-1914

The French concentrated on consolidation in Algeria at the turn of the century, although small parties were constantly venturing deeper and deeper into the Sahara on journeys of exploration. Two companies of the 2e R.E. made an incredible march in April 1900. They set out from Geryville in that month, marched to El Goleah, Timimoun, Laghout, Afloa and returned to Geryville seventy-two days later. This represented a journey of 1,140 miles – an average of 16 miles a day through the terrible terrain of the Great Western Erg, risking death from thirst or massacre in unmapped country. Achievements of a more warlike kind were recorded in 1903 at Doui-Menia and Taghit by the same regiment's Mounted Company, which was involved in clashes along the projected route of the transcontinental railway, which still dominated French thought. Operations around Figuig in that year were notable for a certain lack of co-ordination; the arrival of Col. Lyautey in Oran Province in October saw a firmer direction of the punitive columns, and within three years the desert was peaceful again as far as the Moroccan border.

For many years Morocco had avoided French occupation by skilful diplomacy, but by 1906 France had persuaded Spain and England to ignore her African adventures. The follies of a weak Sultan in Fez played into French hands, and early in 1907 France occupied Oujda, just inside the border; the Mounted Company of the 1er R.E. was with this column. The next step – an advance on Fez – was delayed; roads were inadequate, and a prolonged campaign would have been an embarrassment. Riots in Casablanca gave an excuse for a landing by a force including the 6th Battalion of the 1er R.E.; and French operations settled into a pattern of expansion from that direction into the interior. This was hampered by the tribes, which gathered behind the coastal plain and resisted French incursion with determination. Reinforcements in September 1907 included three battalions of the 2e R.E.; the Legion *régiment de marche* now made up half the strength of the French force. Clashes occurred at Taddert and Sidi Brahim, and October saw an attack on the Muslim centre of Mediouna, some 1,000 *légion-naires* participating. The city was captured, but reoccupied as soon as the French withdrew – a circumstance which attracted the sarcasm of the Press. Gen. Drude mounted a second successful operation in January 1908, but was soon replaced by Gen. d'Amade, who pressed the offensive with vigour and took Settat a few weeks later.

In this campaign the Legion became a favourite of foreign pressmen; the inexorable advance of the hollow square of blue-coated figures, ignoring heavy fire, was an impressive and newsworthy picture. The *légionnaires* were praised in print for their imperturbable steadiness on the battlefield, their markmanship (noticeably superior to French line troops), their discipline, and their cheerful and ingenious improvisation in harsh conditions.

During early 1908 actions were fought at the Mellah River and M'Karto. After resistance eased, most of the *légionnaires* were withdrawn to Algeria. A period of border fighting followed when the Beni Snassen tribe went on the rampage

French infantry tunic, 1899

1908; Legion dead being brought off the field on an artillery limber, on which the bodies of three men may be distinguished. According to the original caption (in a French news magazine) they are a sergent and two légionnaires. (Radio Times Hulton Picture Library)

1908; Legion wounded being carried across the bleak Moroccan plain in mule-panniers. (Radio Times Hulton Picture Library)

July, 1912; a column of the Legion arrives at a camp in Morocco. (Radio Times Hulton Picture Library)

around Geryville. In April a fierce fight at Menabha cost one company 120 casualties, and would have ranked as a disaster had not a traditional Legion bayonet charge retrieved the situation. Another success at Beni Ouzien broke the spirit of the tribes for a while, and for two years only the tirelessly patrolling mounted companies saw scattered action. In April 1911 riots at Fez provided a useful spur, and Gen. Moinier led 35,000 men to 'protect European lives'. One battalion and a mounted company of the Legion took part in the march from Port Lyautey (Kenitra) to Fez, and thereafter the *légionnaires* bore the greatest burden of the blockhouse-building and garrison duty which protected the corridor.

Meanwhile the 6th Battalion of the 1er R.E. was moving west from Algeria; this advance was halted after resistance in the mountain country proved stiffer than anticipated. Morocco became a French protectorate by the Treaty of Fez in March 1912, and this was celebrated by immediate and widespread risings among the tribes. The

Legion played a great part in the fighting which followed, and 1913 saw many battles along the Rabat–Fez axis. The hard core of resistance, the mountainous Tache de Taza, was finally reduced in May–June 1914 by a pincer movement from east and west. *Légionnaires* fought with both armies, and in June a corridor was at last established between Fez and Oujda.

The First World War

On the outbreak of the war the Legion consisted of the two regular regiments, the 1er R.E. at Sidi-bel-Abbes and the 2e R.E. at Saida. Each of these supported a *régiment de marche* in Morocco. Most of the German and Austrian *légionnaires* were transferred to these latter units. A flood of 'duration' foreign volunteers was accepted at recruiting stations in France, and formed into two further *régiments de marche*, each trained and stiffened by

23

cadres of N.C.O.s and veterans from Algeria, and designated 2e Régiment de Marche de 1er Régiment Étranger and 2e Régiment de Marche de 2e Régiment Étranger. (These unwieldy titles will hereafter be abbreviated to 2/1er and 2/2e.) Each of these units, based at Avignon and Toulouse respectively, consisted of three volunteer battalions and one veteran battalion from Algeria. The two types of légionnaire did not mix happily, until the bonds of shared combat were forged.

October 1914 saw these regiments, collectively designated the Legion Brigade and assigned to the Moroccan Division, sent to a quiet sector of the front near Prunay, where they remained until April 1915. In December 1914 a third régiment de marche affiliated to the old 1er R.E. was formed, consisting of three battalions of mainly Italian, Russian and Belgian recruits. Weak in reliable officers and sous-officiers, this 3/1er regiment was posted to Santerre. Both Legion sectors saw scattered fighting, largely confined to patrol clashes and trench raids. The new légionnaires suffered badly from the winter weather. When large drafts from these units were released to their own national armies in March 1915, including groups of several hundred Russians and British, the 3/1er was disbanded.

In November 1914 a 4/1er regiment was formed of Italian volunteers led to France for this purpose by a grandson of Garibaldi: five members of the family served with the three battalions at one time. (Italy, it should be remembered, was not yet involved in the war.) This 4/1er regiment was popularly known as the Garibaldi Brigade, and saw action on Christmas night, 1914, near Bolante in the Argonne region. An attack through wooded country was halted with heavy casualties – the brigade lost 48 dead and 170 wounded. Two days later the Italians attacked once more at Court-Chausses, and managed to take and hold some German positions at a further cost of 125 dead and 172 wounded; among the dead were the Colonel's father, serving as a subaltern, and another member of the Garibaldi family. Further heavy fighting followed in January 1915. By the time Italy entered the war in May 1915 the brigade had lost 429 dead. The survivors rejoined their countrymen to serve in their national army.

The 2/1er saw heavy fighting in May 1915 in the

A group of légionnaires and sous-officers decorated during the First World War. The fighting on the Western Front cost the Legion 115 officers and 5,172 men killed and more than 25,000 wounded. (Radio Times Hulton Picture Library)

Battle of Artois taking some 3,000 yards of German territory in the face of withering fire, but being unable to hold on to what they had gained. Of nearly 4,000 officers and men committed, only some 1,800 remained on their feet after twenty-four hours. The 2/1er was blooded again on 15th June, again near Berthonval Farm, and again without being able to make a significant impression on the German lines.

The 2/2e saw its first major action on 27 September 1915 at Navarin Farm. In two days fighting the 1,600-strong regiment was reduced to 800; incredible feats of courage notwithstanding (the unit was led over open ground under machine-gun fire by a trumpeter blowing the Legion's march, 'Boudin') the regiment was unable to gain more than a matter of yards.

The Moroccan Division was withdrawn from the line in October 1915; by this time the colour of the 2/1er was decorated with the Croix de Guerre and three palms. The following month, in view of dwindling recruiting and heavy casualties, it was decided to fuse all Legion elements in France into the Régiment de Marche de la Légion Étrangère – R.M.L.E. for short. This unit retained its identity for the rest of the war, and stayed with the Moroccan Division. It was of three-battalion strength initially, was commanded by Col. Cot and adopted the colour of the 2/1er.

1 Légionnaire, Grenadier Company, c. 1845
2 Sergent, Voltigeur Company, 1er R.E., 1856
3 Légionnaire, Grenadier Company, 1831

MICHAEL ROFFE

A

1 Légionnaire, Tonkin, 1886
2 Légionnaire, Madagascar, 1900
3 Légionnaire, Grenadier Company,
  Mexico, 1863

B

1 **Légionnaire, Morocco,** *c.* 1908
2 **Lieutenant,** *c.* 1905
3 **Légionnaire, 1re classe,** *c.* 1905

MICHAEL ROFFE

C

1 Légionnaire, 1912
2 Légionnaire, France, 1914
3 Capitaine, 1912

D

1 Caporal, R.L.P.O., Syria, 1930
2 Légionnaire, 1re classe, Algeria, 1939
3 Adjutant-chef, France, 1915

MICHAEL ROFFE

E

1 Adjutant, 1er R.E.P., Algeria, 1960
2 Saharienne, Algeria, 1960
3 Légionnaire, Norway, 1940

F

1 Sergent, 2e R.E.P., 1970
2 Légionnaire drummer, 3e R.E.I., 1970
3 Caporal, 1er R.E., 1970

1 Légionnaire pioneer, 13e D.B.L.E., 1970
2 Capitaine, 3e R.E.I., 1970
3 Légionnaire 1re classe, 2e R.E.P., Tchad, 1970

Committed in the first French Somme offensive, on 4 July 1916, the R.M.L.E. went over the top at Belloy-en-Santerre. They took the village after heavy losses, and held it against two counter-attacks. Another 400 casualties were suffered on 8th July during a further attempt to push the German lines back.

The next major Legion action occurred on 17 April 1917; it was an attack on Auberville in the Sippe Valley. A ghastly struggle in deep mud lasted for no less than six days and nights, during which the Legion expended more than 50,000 grenades alone. Casualties were appalling, and only two kilometres of ground were taken.

In May 1917 the command of the R.M.L.E. passed to Col. Rollet, an extraordinary officer who is still known as 'the Father of the Legion'. (Later a general and the first Inspector-General of the Legion, he was a brave, hot-tempered, slightly eccentric officer who gave his heart and his considerable ability to his unruly charges, who came to regard him with something akin to worship. He died, still the Inspector-General, at Sidi-bel-Abbes in 1941). On Bastille Day 1917, at a large military review in Paris, the President awarded the Médaille Militaire to the colour of the R.M.L.E. – its sixth decoration, making it the most decorated colour in the French Army.

A rather more successful action was fought at Cumiers in August 1917, in which the *légionnaires* took two miles of ground for 350 casualties – cheap, by the standards of 1917. In January 1918 the R.M.L.E. fought in Lorraine, and on 24 April 1918 they played their part in stemming the German spring offensive. Defending an area known as Hangard Wood, they successfully blocked the enemy advance on the Amiens road, at a cost of 850 casualties. In this action all the officers in the leading Legion battalion fell, and one company fought on under the command of a corporal, while another had to place itself in the hands of an experienced *légionnaire*. Between 29th May and 12th June the R.M.L.E. fought around Soissons, and by the collapse of the enemy's spring offensive on that date, this phase of operations had cost the Legion 1,400 casualties. French attacks in late July saw the *légionnaires* well to the fore, taking some eight miles of ground, supported by tanks. They were committed to prolonged attacks on the Hinderburg Line in September, and achieved considerable results, although almost dead from fatigue and down to a strength of about fifty men per company, frequently without a survivor over the rank of sergeant. This attack lasted thirteen days and nights without a pause, and only 700 men of the Legion remained on their feet by the end.

By the close of hostilities the colour of the R.M.L.E. was still among the most decorated in the army. Of 42,883 men who served as *légionnaires* in the European theatre, 6,239 were Frenchmen and the remainder foreigners from over 100 nations. Some 500 officers and 25,000 men were wounded or posted missing, and 115 officers and 5,172 men were killed in action.

A Legion battalion also served with the Régiment de Marche d'Algérie at Gallipoli, later fighting in Serbia. In the spring of 1919 a Legion battalion fought the Red Army as part of the Allied expeditionary force to north Russia.

Africa, 1918-39

Algeria was fairly quiet during the war, but in Morocco the weakened garrisons in the Fez–Oujda corridor and the Fez–Rabat–Casablanca enclave were attacked constantly. One post, Khenifra, was under almost continual siege for four years; and in 1918 some posts had to be abandoned, their retreating garrisons often only barely escaping with their lives. At Gaouz in July 1918 a retreating company screened by a mounted company lost over fifty dead.

A rapid post-war expansion of the Legion was predictable, as a war-torn continent provided thousands of recruits. At Sidi-bel-Abbes and Saida the 1er and 2e Régiments Étranger d'Infanterie retained their identity; the two *régiments de marche* in Morocco were fused into the 4e R.E.I.; and the returning R.M.L.E. became the 3e R.E.I. In 1921 the 1er Régiment Étranger de Cavalerie was formed at Saida, largely from White Russian cavalrymen.

In Morocco the main French line was a series of blockhouses facing north towards the Riff

Colour party of the 1er Régiment Étranger d'Infanterie in the early post-war years. (Radio Times Hulton Picture Library)

Mountains, hotbed of resistance, where the able leader Abd-El-Krim held sway. Educated and astute, Krim had contacts in Europe and provided mercenary training officers for his tribesmen. He had some artillery, and even two aircraft, and staffed his European cadres partly from Legion deserters. (The most famous was a German named Klems, immortalized as 'Odo Klemens' in the stories of P. C. Wren.)

By 1923 French reinforcements had stabilized the blockhouse line in the Taza corridor, and units attempted to push north to widen the pacified strip. This led to furious battles of up to battalion size, and casualties were heavy. Notable Legion actions occurred at Tichoukt, Scoura, El Mers and Ait Maklouf, among other places. The fighting was savage, and the treatment of European prisoners such that every man was careful to carry a last round in his pocket. In April 1924 Krim launched a great attack along the whole length of the corridor, which was repulsed with difficulty. A year later another campaign by his 30,000 men led to 9 French blockhouses being captured and 30 hastily abandoned out of a total

Refreshment halt in the desert, about 1930; a Benigni drawing of a 'two men, one mule' unit of the Legion Mounted Company on campaign

of 66. His unexpected success caused Krim to hesitate, and two fresh Legion battalions were rushed in. Isolated groups linked up, and by June Krim had been contained, at a cost of 3,000 Legion casualties. Notable actions took place at Mediouna, Bibane, Mghala and Aoulai. In May 1926 co-ordinated northward and southward advances on the Riff hinterland by French and

26

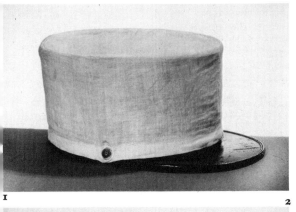

1 The true képi blanc introduced in 1939
2 The képi with the white cover removed, exposing the blue sides, red top and gold badge and strap. On achieving sous-officer rank the cover is permanently discarded. (R. G. Windrow collection)

A less than perfect, but interesting photograph of a soldier of the Legion's great days. Note the tin cup hooked on the side of the canteen. (Radio Times Hulton Picture Library)

A magnificent Benigni drawing of a trooper of the 1er Régiment Étranger de Cavalerie in Syria. A squadron of this regiment conducted the epic defence of Rachaya in November 1925

Spanish troops finally crushed Krim's forces, and he surrendered on 23rd May. All four Legion infantry regiments saw action in this push, as did the new cavalry regiment. The Legion remained in Morocco on garrison and police duties until 1934, dealing with frequent risings.

Syria

Syria was granted to France as a mandate territory after the war, and in 1922 a battalion of the 4e R.E.I. was sent to this new area. The fanatical Druze warriors simmered for three years, and in July 1925 they rose *en masse* and streamed down to the plains. The Legion force moved up-country to block the routes from the hills, fighting their first skirmish at Kafer on 22nd July. The Druze, beaten at Kafer, did better in other areas, and by

August the French forces were in some difficulty. On 16th September the Legion battalion and its attached Mounted Company were attacked at Mousseifré by 3,000 warriors; fighting continued all night and the next day, and had not French aircraft appeared on the afternoon of the 17th the position might have fallen. At least 1,000 casualties were inflicted on the tribesmen for the loss of 47 dead and 83 wounded *légionnaires*.

Another famous action was fought at Rachaya in November 1925. This small hill fort, held by a single squadron of Legion cavalry, was attacked by at least 3,000 warriors on the evening of 20th November. During the night part of the fort was captured, and fighting went on inside the walls for three days, before a desperate bayonet charge cleared the perimeter. Carrier pigeons were sent with appeals for help, but the garrison was down to its last fifteen rounds per man and the grenades had been used up. Half the squadron had become casualties, and the remainder had had no sleep for three days and nights. The commander determined to mount a last Camerone-style charge if help did not appear by the fourth night. Thankfully, the relief column arrived late in the afternoon.

Sporadic fighting went on until the summer of 1927, Messadi and El Chems being names which stand out, but there were no further major battles. The Legion force was raised to a strength of two infantry battalions, a mounted company, and a cavalry squadron, grouped together as the Régiment de la Légion du Proche Orient; with the addition of another infantry battalion in 1936 the R.L.P.O. became the 6e R.E.I.; the designation 5e R.E.I. had gone to the Indo-Chinese garrison force.

The Second World War

October 1933 saw Sidi-bel-Abbes designated the central depot and reception centre for the whole Legion. In 1939 the 2e R.E.C. was formed, mechanized from the start; the 1er R.E.C. had partly converted to patrol vehicles by that stage. The last Mounted Company to give up its mules did not do so until the same year, but most had been transformed into mechanized patrol units. In 1940 the 1er R.E.I. gave birth to the 1e Compagnie Saharienne Port de la Légion, a desert patrol unit which operated in the deep Sahara throughout the Second World War. This C.S.P.L. and its subsequently formed sister units took on the traditions of the old mule companies.

In the years immediately prior to the outbreak of the war the Nazis made efforts to infiltrate agents into the Legion with a view to organizing mutinies among the large number of German N.C.O.s in the event of hostilities. The authorities recognized this, and hundreds of German personnel were interned on the outbreak of war; and there was a natural reluctance to employ the Legion in Europe. To further dilute the possible subversives, some 6,000 'duration only' volunteers were enrolled. Three *régiments de marche* were set up to receive and train volunteers on French soil; the 21er and 22e Régiments de Marche de Volontaires Étrangers were established in October 1939 and the 23e R.M.V.E. in May 1940. The latter, in particular, was an unhappy unit. These R.M.V.E.s contained many Spanish Republicans, and were largely officered by 'dug-out' French reservists.

After due consideration two further units were formed in November 1939 and February 1940 respectively. These were each composed of French volunteers and veteran *légionnaires* from the African units in roughly equal proportions; they were designated the 11e and 12e Régiments Étrangers d'Infanterie. The first true Legion unit formed was Groupement 97, which came into being in North Africa in February 1940. This was drawn from the two Legion cavalry regiments, and eventually comprised four squadrons of armoured cars; it moved to France in March 1940. Last, but most famous of all, the 13e Demi-Brigade Légion Étrangère appeared in early 1940. Drawn from volunteer *légionnaires* of all units, it was intended for service with the Finnish forces. The Finns were defeated while the unit was still undergoing mountain training in France, and it was therefore sent instead to Norway, landing on 6 May 1940.

On 28 May 1940 the 13e D.B.L.E. went into action at Narvik. It held up the German advance in its sector with great success, although outnumbered; one and a half companies were lost by

REGIMENTAL BADGES
(Left to right)
The Cross of Lorraine distinguishes the badge of the 13e Demi-Brigade, the Free French unit of the Legion which fought at Narvik, Bir Hacheim and in Europe

Post-war badge of the 2e R.E.I., the dragon in obvious reference to service in Indo-China, 1946–54. The red grenade and number are superimposed on the gold dragon on an emerald-green enamel base, picked out in gold

'The Legion is our home-land' – motto on the badge of the 3e R.E.I.

(R. G. Windrow collection)

the time the Anglo-French forces were evacuated. The unit returned to Brest. Early in June it went into action near Rennes, and when the cease-fire was declared Col. Magrin-Vernerey gave his men the choice of taking ship for England and offering their services to de Gaulle, or remaining in France. About half the unit followed him to England. (On arrival he designated this force, briefly, as the 14e D.B.L.E., but they reverted to their old title – which they have held ever since – when it was learned that the part which had remained in France had been disbanded by the Vichy command.)

Meanwhile, the other 'Legion' units and Groupement 97 had suffered varying fortunes. Between 27th May and 11th June the 11e R.E.I. offered a stubborn defence at Inor Wood between the Meuse and the Chiers. Reduced to half strength, they then joined the general retreat, and disappeared in the chaos of defeat. The colour was burned rather than allowed to fall into enemy hands. The 12e R.E.I. was committed on 6th June near Soissons, and reduced to one-third strength in thirty-six hours; few broke out of the German encirclement. The 21er R.M.V.E. broke under heavy attack in the Ardennes on 10th June, and were not employed again. The 22e R.M.V.E. did rather better near Peronne, but German infantry and armour smashed the unit in a three-day battle which cost the regiment half its strength. The unready 23e R.M.V.E., without proper

equipment, delayed enemy armour for two days near Soissons, but had to fall back on 17th June. Groupement 97 made contact in the Somme area on 18th May, and fought courageous delaying actions for the next three weeks. Galled by constant retreat, the *légionnaires* mounted a furious counter-attack against German tanks on 9th June. It was Camerone on wheels; half the obsolete armoured cars were destroyed in minutes. Ignoring a chance to retreat, the survivors charged again, and were annihilated.

Under the Vichy Government, the Legion became subject to checks by a German commission; these were usually circumvented by sending such *légionnaires* as were likely to attract German attention out on long training marches when the inspection was imminent. 'Wanted' *légionnaires* were quietly shipped off to the 5e R.E.I. in Indo-China. The 4e R.E.I., redesignated 4e Demi-Brigade, was filled out with men anxious to avoid German scrutiny and shipped to Senegal. The 1er R.E.I. remained at Sidi-bel-Abbes, much reduced, while the 2e R.E.I. was disbanded. The 3e R.E.I. remained in Morocco on garrison duty, the 1er R.E.C. continued to operate at reduced strength, and the 2e R.E.C. was disbanded. Surviving units settled into dull desert garrison duty, enlivened by an apparently popular game of 'cat-and-mouse' with the German inspection board. A number of German *légionnaires*, eventually totalling 2,000, were removed by the Germans and formed into a special unit of the Wehrmacht, the Afrika Korps's 361st Infantry Regiment.

Vichy treatment of 'duration only' *légionnaires* who demanded their release was savage. Many died in grim desert labour camps, whose reputation has unfairly been applied to the Legion itself by later critics.

The 13ᵉ D.B.L.E. in England was brought to a strength of two battalions, and in December 1940 was used in the French Cameroons. It was then shipped to Port Sudan in February 1941, and fought alongside British and Empire troops at Keren and Massawa. On 8 June 1941 a joint force of British and Free French crossed from Jordan into Vichy Syria, and the 13ᵉ D.B.L.E. was part of the column which headed for Damascus. A tragic episode followed. The main resistance was provided by the 6ᵉ R.E.I., and at Damas in the Syrian hills *légionnaire* met *légionnaire* in a bitter struggle. Casualties on both sides were heavy, but the attitude was very definitely one of '*Légionnaire* first, enemy second' when it came to the treatment of wounded and prisoners. There are many recorded examples of an almost eighteenth-century courtesy between foes in this campaign, although in actual combat there was no slackening of vigour on either side. The more modern equipment of the 13ᵉ probably won the day. When Syria was turned over to the Free French the 6ᵉ R.E.I. was disbanded; some 1,000 men joined the 13ᵉ D.B.L.E. as a third battalion, but only two of the French officers.

The able and popular ex-Georgian prince, Col. Amilakvari, a Legion veteran since 1924, took command of the 13ᵉ D.B.L.E. in August 1941. He led it in February 1942 to Bir Hacheim in the Western Desert, where a Free French defensive position formed the southern point of the Eighth Army's lines. On 27 May 1942 Italian armour attacked the Legion positions; by nightfall thirty-two of the tanks had been destroyed, and the Legion was still firmly established. On 2nd June a major armoured assault by the Afrika Korps began, with air support. For nine days the *légionnaires* and Free French units held out against incessant pressure, and then slipped out without mishap on the night of 10th June; the battle had reduced the 13ᵉ D.B.L.E. to two battalions. The *légionnaires* were heavily committed at El Himeimat

Sketch of the command half-track, named 'Camerone', of the 13ᵉ Demi-Brigade's 7th Company in north-west Europe in 1944

– on the extreme left flank of the El Alamein line – on 23 October 1942, when Col. Amilakvari was killed at the head of his men. The Legion unit remained with the Eighth Army all the way to Tunisia.

When the Anglo-American forces landed at Oran on 8 November 1942 the 1ᵉʳ R.E.I. was ordered to resist, but deliberately 'dragged its feet' until the Vichy forces capitulated. When the final battles in Tunisia began, the North African regiments and the 4ᵉ D.B.L.E. (hastily recalled from Senegal) raised two *régiments de marche* to fight with the Allies, the 1ᵉʳ and 3ᵉ R.E.I.M. The Legion cavalry formed a mechanized combat group, the Groupe Autonome. This latter unit captured a German position at Foum El Gouafel on 11 January 1943, without fatal casualties. The 3ᵉ R.E.I.M. was too eager to get into the battle for Kasserine Pass, and got into difficulties at Jebel Mansour. The 1ᵉʳ R.E.I.M. was also committed, with the British First Army, and despite 300 casualties was eventually successful. Meanwhile the 13ᵉ D.B.L.E. was advancing from Libya, and was reduced to 1,200 men by a two-day battle, victorious but costly, against the German 90th Light Division at Djebel Garci in February. The 1ᵉʳ R.E.I.M. was now issued with modern weapons and saw action at Pont du Fahs and

Zaghouan in May. After the German capitulation, the German regiment of ex-*légionnaires* was interned; in 1945 many were allowed to rejoin the Legion.

Legion strength in North Africa was well below 10,000 by this stage, so the remnants were formed into the second R.M.L.E. in thirty years; mounted in half-tracks, with the 1er R.E.C. in armoured cars, they provided the mechanized infantry for an armoured division. The 13e D.B.L.E. remained independent, and joined the Fifth Army in Italy in April 1944, where it fought with distinction before Rome. It landed at Cavalaire in southern France on 16 August 1944, and fought near Toulon and Lyons. In September it was joined in France by the R.M.L.E. and R.E.C., serving with the 5th Moroccan Division. The *légionnaires* distinguished themselves particularly at Belfort in November 1944, on the Rhine, and at Colmar in February 1945. Both the R.M.L.E. and 13e D.B.L.E. took part in the capture of the latter. The Legion forged on to the east, and fought at Stuttgart and Friedrichshafen before the end of the war found them at Arlberg in Austria.

Indo-China, 1941-54

In return for granting facilities in Indo-China in 1941 the Vichy administration were allowed by the victorious Japanese to retain nominal internal control of the country. The existence of the 5e R.E.I. for the next three years was frustrating in the extreme; and when Japan ordered the disarming and internment of French troops in March 1945 the remaining 3,000 men, goaded by the brutal treatment of units which resisted this order, assembled and began a fighting retreat into Yunnan. The 500-mile jungle march was an epic of endurance, and it was only after fighting their way through numerous Japanese ambushes that the Legion force crossed the border fifty-two days later. They remained in China during the Japanese withdrawal and subsequent power vacuum, when Ho Chi Minh declared the independent state of Vietnam. When France landed troops at Hanoi in April 1946 they marched back,

but so many men were time-expired that the regiment was soon disbanded.

The enormous political complexity of this situation crystallized into guerilla warfare between France and the Viet Minh rebels in 1946; the latter were determined and well equipped, and the long-drawn agonies of post-colonial warfare began. The Legion were heavily committed to this bitter, and mismanaged campaign, and was soon swollen with men from P.O.W. cages and displaced persons camps all over Europe and the East. The first contingent to arrive was the revived 2e R.E.I., which lost 230 men in its first three months of duty in southern Annam in February–May 1946. In March 1946 the 13e D.B.L.E. arrived, and spent the next two years in the swamps of Cochin Chine. The 3e R.E.I., reborn from the wartime R.M.L.E., landed in June. The Sidi-bel-Abbes training depot was now turned into a vast soldier-factory, run by the 1er R.E.I., to feed the Indo-Chinese theatre.

No purpose can be served by a detailed history

In French Indo-China in 1954 the Legion suffered its bitterest defeat at Dien Bien Phu

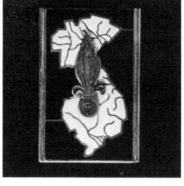

REGIMENTAL BADGES

The now defunct 4e R.E.I. wore this badge, charged with the Legion colours of red and green, the seven-flamed grenade, and a Moslem minaret

The map of Indo-China provides the basis for the badge of the 5e R.E.I. Many volunteers from this regiment made a desperate parachute drop (without previous experience) into Dien Bien Phu shortly before the fall of the fortress

The badge of the 1er B.E.P., later the 1er R.E.P. The heroic tradition founded in Indo-China ended tragically with the Generals' revolt of 1961

The 2e R.E.P., which was air-dropped into Dien Bien Phu. This unit has recently seen action in the Republic of Tchad

(R. G. Windrow collection)

of the war; its pattern is all too familiar in 1971. Guerrilla raids led to guerrilla control of all country not immediately under the vigilance of garrison towns. The roads became unsafe at nightfall; then, unsafe at any time except in armed convoys which were frequently attacked or mined. Isolated posts were overrun, and small but heroic last stands and ambush skirmishes became commonplace. The Viet Minh leader, Gen. Giap, built up his strength and the confidence of his men, husbanding his regular units until they were fit to take on the French in pitched battles on ground of their own choosing.

Legion units which fought in Indo-China included the 1er R.E.C., which disembarked its light armour in January 1947, and was split into combat groups for road patrol duties. The 3e R.E.I. left Cochin Chine in March 1947, and moved into Tonkin where it manned a number of posts commanding the ridges which fan out from the delta towards the Chinese border. In November 1948 the first Legion airborne unit, the 1er Bataillon Etranger Parachutiste arrived at Saigon,

and was soon followed by the 2e B.E.P. In November 1949 the revived 5e R.E.I. appeared in Tonkin.

A few notable actions should be mentioned. In July 1948 a fort at Phu Tong Hoa was defended by 104 men of the 3e R.E.I. against night-long attacks by large Viet Minh forces with mortar support. The relief column arrived to find that the garrison had beaten off the attack by its own resources, suffering 53 casualties in the process. The senior surviving N.C.O. turned out the guard, in ceremonial uniform, to present arms to the relief force commander. On 12 May 1949 the 1er B.E.P. was at the head of a force which threw the Viet Minh out of the old Black Flag fort and Legion post of Tuyen Quang, first stormed by *légionnaires* in 1884! In September 1950 Giap began his move to drive the French from Tonkin, and the forts commanding the ridges above the Delta were a priority target. Dong Khe, a sandbagged post held by two companies of the 3e R.E.I., was singled out; it was encircled on 16th September, and shelled all day by Giap's Chinese artillery.

At dusk under covering mortar fire, the six Viet Minh battalions attacked; and by the second night they had inflicted 140 casualties and driven the *légionnaires* out of three of the four sandbagged bastions. During the night a counter-attack recaptured another of the strongpoints, which then changed hands a further seven times before dawn found the Viets once more in possession. In the morning the last strongpoint was set on fire, and the last few *légionnaires* went out in a bayonet charge. A handful of survivors made their way through the jungle to the nearest French post with the story. Two relief columns – the rest of the 3e R.E.I. from Kao-Bang, and the 1er B.E.P. from Lang-Son – were ambushed and badly mauled. Two Legion battalions were written off during this period, and while covering the retreat to the Red River the 1er B.E.P. suffered 90 per cent casualties.

The French eventually took the misjudged decision to dig in and lure Giap into positional warfare, unaware of the progress he had made in training conventional divisional formations and the size of his artillery force. The dusty bowl-shaped valley of Dien Bien Phu was chosen, and secured by air-dropped paratroopers of the 1er B.E.P. in November 1953; it was completely surrounded by enemy territory from the start. By January 1954 the twelve-battalion garrison included seven Legion battalions drawn from the 13e D.B.L.E., the 2e and 3e R.E.I., and the 1er B.E.P. The position was built up into a strong series of interlocking but self-contained bastions, with fixed lines of fire and mutual artillery support. Each strongpoint was code-named with a girl's name (see sketch map).

Giap accepted the challenge; four divisions encircled the 14,000-man garrison, carrying their dismantled artillery and anti-aircraft guns over the steep jungle tracks. So numerous and accurate were the latter that French air cover was virtually neutralized. By 11 January 1954 the isolation of the garrison was almost complete, and the airstrip was only kept open with difficulty. The tightening ring of Viet forces sapped inwards across the valley floor, and by early March Legion patrols were severely restricted. On 13th March the first major artillery barrage smashed on to dug-outs built to withstand only mortar fire, and huge waves of

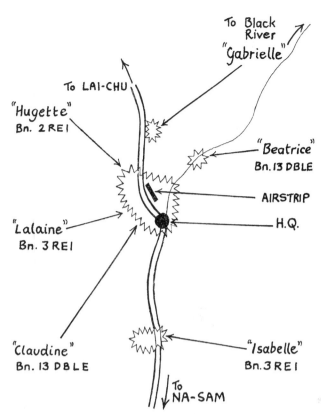

Dien Bien Phu, 1954. The bastions, each code-named with a girl's name, were interlocking but self-contained, with fixed lines of fire and mutual artillery support

infantry fell on the bastion of *Beatrice*, held by men of the 13e D.B.L.E., and also on *Gabrielle* and *Isabelle*. These latter held out, but *Beatrice* fell, with 400 Legion casualties. Fierce attacks on 25th March cost the French part of *Lalaine*; by this time the fire was so heavy and constant that the garrison was forced underground during daylight. Attacks between 30th March and 4th April ended with the Viets established close to the airstrip, rendering it useless.

Constant artillery fire and mass night attacks shrunk the perimeter. On the night of 9th April the 2e B.E.P. was air-dropped into the fortress, and on succeeding nights several hundred volunteers from the 3e and 5e R.E.I. made their first parachute jumps over Dien Bien Phu. The final assault began on 6 May 1954. Accepting massive casualties the Viets swarmed over the wire, and by daybreak only the isolated *Isabelle*, and a small area around the H.Q. remained in French hands. The next night the last attacks went in, and just before dawn on 8th May the fortress fell. At *Isabelle* survivors of a battalion of the 3e R.E.I.

held out for some hours after the H.Q. radio went off the air; then, after smashing everything of value, they went out over the wire in a last wild bayonet charge. They are thought to have got about 150 yards.

The Indo-Chinese war cost the Foreign Legion 314 officers and 10,168 men dead, and three times that number of wounded.

Algeria

Little purpose can be served by describing in detail the anti-F.L.N. operations to which the Legion was committed during Algeria's war of independence. There was no single significant battle; the familiar pattern of this type of war does not give rise to pitched battles. Suffice it to say that the Legion bore the brunt of ground operations, and that the brutality of this type of warfare was displayed equally by French and Algerian alike.

Six Legion infantry regiments[6], two cavalry, and two parachute regiments fought in Algeria. The 1er R.E.I. at Sidi-bel-Abbes retained its role as the main reception and training formation, and mounted operations in its immediate locality. The 2e R.E.I., completely motorized, patrolled southern Oran Province from Ain Sefra and Geryville. The 3e R.E.I. was based in Kabylia, and the 4e R.E.I. operated near the Tunisian Barrage from 1958 onwards. The 5e R.E.I. was based around Tlemcen and Arzew, and the 13e D.B.L.E. fought in the Aures Mountains. Both cavalry regiments, equipped with American and French armoured cars, patrolled the Tunisian Barrage from Tebessa. 1955 saw both parachute battalions expanded to regimental strength: the 1er R.E.P. was based at Zeralda and the 2e R.E.P. at Philippeville. The colourful *Saharienne* companies – raised in 1940, 1946, 1949 and 1955 respectively – continued their traditional 'mule company' operations as deep penetration patrol units.

A tragic postscript to the Algerian war was the revolt of four French generals and some of the best combat units, incensed over the decision to grant independence to the country they had fought to pacify. The 1er R.E.P. was deeply involved in this

Legion paratrooper's beret badge. The green beret is much worn in the field by all types of Legion unit. Men of other than airborne formations wear a cap badge depicting the Legion's seven-flamed grenade in a pierced circle. (R. G. Windrow collection)

unhappy affair, and was disbanded on 28 April 1961. Officers of other Legion regiments were brought to trial, and a general, understandable, but unjustified mistrust hastened the inevitable running down of Legion strength after hostilities ceased.

More than 1,200 *légionnaires* died in action against the F.L.N.

The Legion Today

Now back in official and public favour, the Legion has shrunk in size with the disappearance of the French overseas empire, but has been brought up to an unprecedented level of equipment and training as a balanced modern force of professional soldiers spread among motorized and helicopter-borne infantry, paratroopers, and light armour. All ancillary services are manned by *légionnaires*, and specialist cadres – frogmen, demolition teams, Arctic warfare experts, and so forth – exist in great numbers. Its semi-independent position within the armed forces is analogous to that of the U.S. Marine Corps. Current strength is thought to be at divisional level – between 12,000 and 15,000 men.

The 1er Régiment Étranger, now at Aubagne near Marseilles, is the depot, training and administrative centre.

The 2e Régiment Étranger d'Infanterie remained in Algeria until 1968 at the Reggan and Colomb Bechar training areas, and was then disbanded.

The 3e Régiment Étranger d'Infanterie has for several years been based at Diego Suarez in Madagascar.

The 5e Régiment Mixte du Pacifique, a specialist and technical unit, is based on Tahiti, where it has carried out much useful construction work; it is also believed to serve a function connected with missile-testing areas.

The 13e D.B.L.E. operates as motorized infantry from Djibouti in the Côte Française des Somalis.

The 1er Régiment Étranger de Cavalerie, now the only cavalry unit, is based at Orange in the south of France, with Panhard EBR-75 and EBR-90 heavy armoured cars and AMX-13 light tanks.

The 2e Régiment Étranger Parachutiste has a base at Calvi in Corsica. Strong drafts have been on active service in the Republic of Tchad for nearly two years; the government of this ex-French possession have invoked defence agreements to counter insurgency by some 80,000 nomadic tribesmen.

The C.S.P.L.s have been reabsorbed into the motorized infantry units as compagnies portées, while retaining their traditional insignia. In addition, each regiment has an armoured reconnaissance element, currently equipped with British Ferret scout cars, some mounting large-calibre recoilless weapons.

The 'ideological' training of légionnaires remains remarkably similar to that followed a century ago. Carrying the most modern weapons and equipment, and spending all but a few days of his year in camouflage suit and green beret rather than white képi and fringed epaulettes, the légionnaire is still indoctrinated with the ideals of Camerone, and made to feel very much a part of an extraordinary tradition of professional soldiering. The men of the Légion Étrangère still take a fierce pride in belonging – belonging very completely – to a corps which can be counted upon to do the impossible when others have failed, or to die, uncomplaining, in the attempt.

NOTES

1. The original battalion establishment was eight companies each of 112 men commanded by a captain. The Legion was ahead of its time in that from the outset its battalions included two compagnies d'élite (see explanatory note, 3. below), a practice not yet adopted by the majority of the French line regiments.

2. The bataillon de marche, and later the régiment de marche, figured in the history of the Legion's campaigns with great frequency. These were ad hoc 'task groups' formed of men detached from the parent units, which maintained a skeleton establishment and unit identity at the home depot while a number – sometimes an overwhelming majority – of their companies were on campaign hundreds or thousands of miles away. At periods when the Legion consisted of more than one regiment the bataillon de marche might be linked directly by title and organization with a particular parent formation; at other times this practice was not followed. In the years before 1868 such task groups were often formed from the compagnies d'élite; see below.

3. The compagnies d'élite of a French regiment prior to 1868 – when the system was abandoned – consisted of compagnies grenadiers and compagnies voltigeurs. The remaining sub-units were referred to as 'companies of the centre'. Basically the grenadiers, distinguished by red trimmings to the uniform, were the shock assault force, and the voltigeurs, distinguished by yellow, were the light infantry or skirmishing line. Officially each battalion had one company of each category, but in the Legion of the 1840s and 1850s it sometimes happened that a battalion might support as many as four compagnies d'élite. In 1835, when the 'New Legion' was formed, it did not include compagnies d'élite, but the privilege was restored after the taking of Constantine in 1837.

4. It was during this period that the establishment of a Legion battalion was reduced to four companies each of about 120 men; average battalion strength in the 1870s and 1880s seems to have been about 600 men.

5. At about this time the strength of a Legion battalion seems to have stabilized at some 800 men.

6. In 1957 the organization of légionnaires into battalions was abandoned. Each regiment has since then consisted of ten companies; the proportion of pure rifle companies to specialist companies (mortar, reconnaissance, light armour, headquarters, etc.) has decreased steadily as modern equipment became available.

The Plates

A1 Légionnaire of Grenadier Company, Algeria, c. 1845
The red cloth cap (*casquette d'Afrique*) appeared during the conquest of Algeria in about 1840, and several models with minor variations, such as the squaring of the peak, came into use as the century progressed. The 1822 model grey double-breasted greatcoat is worn buttoned back for ease of movement, and at this early stage the practice of wearing it in the field, whatever the conditions and if necessary without the tunic or shirt beneath it, had already been noted. The crossbelts supporting bayonet and cartridge pouch have been abandoned in favour of black leather harness, and a large pouch with the grenadier badge painted on the flap is worn centrally at the front – a long-lasting custom of the Legion, who retained this style after it had been superseded in other units. The all-red fringed epaulettes also indicate a grenadier. The trousers are worn tucked into the white gaiters when in the field. A tan cloth tent section and a tent pole are attached to the pack. The percussion musket was issued in about 1842.

A2 Sergent of Voltigeur Company, 1er R.E., 1856
The Swiss Regiment raised for service in the Crimea, which became the 1er Régiment Étranger and was shipped to Algeria in 1856, were dressed initially in a rifle-green uniform, which is thought to have been replaced by Legion blue and red as new garments became necessary between 1856 and 1859. The green shako with yellow distinctions is basically the 1856 model, and in any other regiment the soldier illustrated would wear the double yellow pompoms of a *voltigeur* when on parade. The brass chin scales date from 1855, and the eagle shako plate from 1852. The three-quarter length coatee is the standard French Army 1845 issue; the greatcoat, now of a blue-grey shade, is strapped round the pack. Yellow epaulettes and a yellow hunting horn on the collar also refer to the *voltigeur* function, and these companies appear to have been issued with the yellow-striped blue-grey trousers of the *chasseurs à pied* in place of the red of centre and grenadier companies. The gold

oblique stripe on each forearm is the rank badge of a *sergent*. This *voltigeur* is equipped with the brass-hilted sabre bayonet, another mark of distinction from the centre and grenadier companies. The pouch is worn at the back – when this regiment was absorbed into the Legion proper it is likely that it was moved to the front to conform with unit custom. The individual mess-tin or *gamelle* carried on top of the pack was introduced in December 1852, and tin mugs were frequently carried in some handy position on the belt or harness.

A3 Légionnaire of Grenadier Company, Algeria, 1831
The first *légionnaire*. The shako is the 1825 model with red grenadier distinctions; the tricolour cockade is thought to have been introduced in 1830. It should be noted that one of the peculiarities of the Legion was the early abandonment of the double pompoms worn by *compagnies d'élite* of other units – double red pompoms indicating grenadiers, double yellow indicating *voltigeurs*. The short jacket or coatee is basically the 1822 model with red grenadier distinctions and epaulettes; the red collar was, however, common to all infantry from 1828 onward. The trousers, in *garance* (madder red) replaced the blue winter and white summer trousers worn up to 1829. The striped cloth case on top of the pack contained the grey 1822 model greatcoat. The musket is a flintlock; percussion arms did not appear in any numbers until the early 1840s.

B1 Légionnaire, Tonkin, 1886
This soldier wears the 1878 model *casque colonial* with a white canvas cover; Tonkin saw the first issue of this helmet to the Legion, and it was also used in Dahomey, the Sudan, Madagascar and even by some units in Algeria, largely those based in the southern wilderness of Oran Province. No spare clothing stocks accompanied the Legion to Indo-China, a typical example of neglect. Before many months had passed in that humid climate many units were forced to draw on stocks of Infanterie de Marine uniform, and this *légionnaire* wears an 1873 model tunic of that service, double-breasted, with two rows of seven buttons; the *marsouin* collar insignia have been removed. The standard madder-red trousers are still worn here; as stocks ran out they were replaced by *marsouin*

white drill. The Legion's blue sash is worn under the belt and equipment, and the white canvas Negrier cartridge pouch is worn across the chest; this saw use in the Legion's tropical service regiments for a few years at the end of the last century, and was designed by the general of that name for the convenience of men forced to load while in the prone position. The long white gaiters were officially withdrawn in 1881, but the Legion always lagged behind regular units in such matters and was very much a law unto itself. The rifle is the Le Gras model.

B2 Légionnaire, Madagascar, 1900

The soldier illustrated is serving with one of the companies which returned to Madagascar to put down prolonged rebellions at the turn of the century. In fact the only way in which he differs from those involved in the original invasion is in the gaiters; the short, laced black leather model was first issued in 1900, prior to which the trousers were simply gathered at the ankle and tied, or allowed to fall free over the ankle-boot. The humidity and heat of this region led to a general adoption of shirt-sleeve order in the field, although the steel blue-grey *capote* is carried on the pack, as are pots and pans, spare boots and bivouac poles. The Negrier pouch is still worn, together with the two leather belt pouches for Lebel ammunition. The white shirt and trousers of coarse linen or canvas are standard Legion fatigue issue.

B3 Légionnaire of Grenadier Company, Mexico, 1863

One of the several *casquettes d'Afrique* is worn, with a white cloth cover and neck protector – this was widely used in the Mexican campaign. The large straw sombrero was worn initially, but was very unpopular and frequently abandoned in favour of the cap. The tunic is the *habit-tunique* of 1860 issue, with the yellow collar common to all infantry and red grenadier epaulettes and distinctions. The short, full white trousers worn with fawn leather *jambières* and white gaiters were also of 1860 issue, copied from the style worn for some years previously by Imperial Guard *chasseurs à pied*. The pouch of cartridges for the Minié rifle is worn in front by the *légionnaire*. Two items are of interest. The red sash was certainly worn by grenadiers and the blue sash by centre companies;

it may be assumed that *voltigeurs* wore yellow sashes. When the *compagnies d'élite* were abolished in 1868 the Legion continued to wear the blue sash which they had acquired in Mexico, and wear it to this day. Epaulettes of grenadiers, *voltigeurs* and centre troops were red fringed, yellow fringed, and green with red crescent but no fringe, respectively. After 1868 all *légionnaires* wore green epaulettes with a full red fringe; and the other grenadier distinction, the grenade badge itself, became the insignia of the Legion. Authentication for these practices is not available at present, and it is possible that the Legion simply 'acquired' these items, making the most of the unit's isolation from Paris and the indifference with which it was regarded by the military authorities for many years.

C1 Légionnaire, Morocco, c. 1908

This soldier might be termed 'the classic *légionnaire*'. He wears the standard campaign dress and equipment of the Legion in North Africa. The *képi* is worn with a cover, originally khaki (since *c.* 1880), but bleached almost white by sun and frequent scrubbing, and a white neck protector; this latter was never official issue, but was much worn at various periods from the 1850s until the 1920s. The *capote* of steel blue-grey is worn over a shirt or next to the skin, the flaps buttoned back for ease of marching. The white fatigue trousers were often worn in the field, and no rigid regulation seems to have covered when the red or white patterns might be used; both were frequently observed. The blue sash is wrapped round the waist under the leather harness, and two leather ammunition pouches are worn on the belt. The canteen or *bidon* is covered with *capote* cloth laced in position. A white scarf worn as illustrated was popular but not official issue. The red chevrons on the left upper arm indicate long service and good conduct. The tan cloth tent section is strapped round the pack, and bivouac poles are carried; the *légionnaire* in the field often added bundles of kindling to his burdens, and, not infrequently, such small game or domestic animals as could be potted on the march or 'liberated' from Arab herds and villages. The Lebel rifle is carried with 'Rosalie' – the *epée* bayonet – fixed; for decades it was the *légionnaire's* favourite weapon.

C2 Lieutenant, grande tenue de service, c. 1905

This officer's uniform is almost identical to that worn throughout the army. The single lines of gold piping on the *képi* indicate rank; double piping was worn by captains, and triple by officers from *commandant* upwards. The black tunic bears standard rank distinctions on the cuffs, and one fringed gold epaulette on the left shoulder balanced by an unfringed epaulette on the right is also an indication of rank. The black belt and crossbelt support the 1892 model revolver and holster, and the 1882 model nickel-plated sabre is carried. Cuff stripes at this time depended to some extent on the unit; it is thought that the sequence followed in the Legion was one gold stripe for *adjutant* (senior warrant officer) and *sous-lieutenant*; two for *lieutenant*; three for *capitaine* and *commandant major*; three gold and one silver for *chef bataillon*; three gold and two silver for *lieutenant-colonel*; and five gold for *colonel*.

C3 Légionnaire de première classe, walking-out dress, c. 1905

The model 1886 *képi*, red with blue piping and a red grenade badge, is worn by this junior N.C.O. without a cloth cover when in walking-out dress. The 1899 model tunic bears the unique green and red Legion epaulettes and the red oblique rank stripe of a *légionnaire de première classe*; two red stripes indicated *caporal*, and a single gold stripe, *sergent*. The red collar and regimental numbers are in line with general army practice of that time, as are the madder-red trousers, worn over a short white spat for walking out. The bayonet is the *épée* pattern used with the Lebel rifle.

D1 Légionnaire, fatigue dress, c. 1912

The coarse white baggy shirt and trousers were worn, with the sash, as fatigue and undress uniform by *légionnaires* from about 1870 until after the First World War. Note the *képi* cover retains some of its original khaki colouring.

D2 Légionnaire, France, 1914

This illustration was prepared from a photograph of an American who joined the Legion in France in 1914. The single-breasted *capote* with breast pockets was sometimes issued from army stocks. The *képi* was worn with a blue-grey cloth cover by all French troops after the initial engagements of the war; otherwise the uniform and equipment is virtually identical to that worn for thirty years.

D3 Capitaine, c. 1912

The dress worn by Legion officers in the field was more varied and less stringently regulated than that of the troops, and personal choice and finance tended to be important factors. This captain, identifiable by the double piping on the crown of the *képi*, is in fact wearing an issue garment; the black infantry officer's *pèlerine* or cape coat, with buttoned-on hood, was one of several expedients frequently adopted to combat the freezing desert night. The use of puttees in place of knee boots by officers in the field was not uncommon.

E1 Caporal, Régiment de Légion du Proche Orient, Syria, c. 1930

The lightweight linen drill uniform illustrated here, worn with puttees to the knee, was issued gradually during the inter-war years and was worn both in the field and in barracks. For parade purposes white leather or canvas belts, pouches and harness were worn over the blue sash. The tunic was usually worn next to the skin and open at the neck, and white scarves were common. The double green chevron above the buttoned cuff is the insignia of a *caporal*. Note that the low, crushed-looking *képi* with a semi-bleached cover is still worn.

E2 Légionnaire de première classe, Algeria, 1939

The most striking point about this figure is the appearance in this year of the stiffened cylindrical *képi* with a true white cover – the first appearance of the *képi blanc* which has become the trade mark of the Legion. The khaki greatcoat carried since the end of the First World War is worn, with a green grenade badge on the lapels. Under it is worn the linen uniform illustrated in E1. The leather equipment has not changed, and a white scarf is worn, knotted in the characteristic fashion. The red chevron on the left arm is a long-service and good-conduct distinction, the single green chevron on both cuffs, the mark of rank. (A trivial but intriguing point: this figure was prepared from a photograph of 1939, and a picture published in 1969, showing a Legion paratrooper in Tchad, includes a white scarf knotted in exactly this fashion – obviously a minor Legion tradition.)

E3 Adjutant-chef, R.M.L.E., France, 1915

The realities of trench warfare necessitated the rapid abandonment of the colourful but impractical French infantry uniform, which was replaced by the horizon-blue uniform among regular infantry and by a khaki uniform of similar cut among colonial troops. The Legion was issued with the latter, but there was a transitional period when horizon blue was worn. The Adrian helmet was standard issue. The senior warrant officer illustrated here bears a single rank stripe above the cuffs of his coat, and five red long-service and good-conduct chevrons on the left upper arm. The belt, crossbelt, leggings and revolver holster are all worn exactly as with officers' uniform, and the gold grenade badges woven diagonally on each side of the tunic collar are also characteristic of warrant and commissioned officers alike. The embossed grenade on the front of the helmet bears no relationship to the Legion insignia; it was worn on all French Army helmets.

F1 Adjutant, 1er Régiment Étranger Parachutiste, Algeria, 1960

The paratroop units of the Legion, the 1er and 2e R.E.P., bore a heavy burden during the fighting in Algeria. This senior warrant officer – his rank identified by the white-on-midnight-blue stripe slipped over his shoulder straps – wears the standard French camouflaged bush shirt and trousers, with capacious pockets. The light webbing equipment is strung with magazine pouches for the P.M. submachine-gun, grenades and canteens. The green beret appeared during the late 1950s, and is worn with hanging tapes and the French paratrooper's cap badge (see photograph, p. 34). This same beret was issued to certain infantry formations before the close of the Algerian War and now, with the Legion's grenade in a pierced circle as the cap badge, is standard issue and peculiar to the Legion; it is worn in the field and as working dress. This N.C.O. carries the standard army helmet with camouflaged cloth cover.

F2 Légionnaire, Compagnies Sahariennes Port de la Légion, 1960

The traditions of an earlier age of desert patrolling are commemorated in the uniform of the *Saharienne*. This colourful dress, obviously worn only on parade, has an affinity with the imitations of native clothing so popular in the mid-nineteenth century – for instance, the Zouave and Spahi regiments. The post-war Legion arm badge is worn on the left upper arm; a green grenade on a black diamond in a triple green edging. The normal Legion parade epaulettes are worn. The insignia on the trousers reflects the shape of the various C.S.P.L. unit badges, worn in metal on a leather fob hanging from the button of the right breast pocket. The uniform of each of the four C.S.P.L.s varied in slight details from the others. Officers and senior N.C.O.s wore white belted tunics with full-length sleeves on parade occasions. The rifle is the standard French Army F.S.A. 49/56 semi-automatic.

F3 Légionnaire, 13e Demi-Brigade Légion Étrangère, Norway, 1940

This soldier wears the standard French Army khaki-painted Adrian helmet in use at the beginning of the Second World War, and winter warfare equipment issued when it was intended to send this volunteer formation to fight in Finland. This was retained when the 13e D.B.L.E. was diverted to Narvik. The 'knickerbocker' trousers and mountain boots with double socks were still worn when the remnants of this unit escaped to England.

No other Second World War uniforms have been included in the colour section. On arrival in England, or shortly thereafter, the Legion was equipped from British Army stocks. Legion badges of rank were worn on British battledress, and later, when Legion units moved to North Africa, on Eighth Army desert uniform. The *képi* was retained, where available. In north-west Europe and Italy in 1943 and 1944, United States Army uniforms with Legion badges were universally worn; small arms and transport also came from American sources. The Vichy regiments which remained in the Middle East continued to wear the pre-war linen uniform until their disbandment.

In the first great post-war campaign in which the Legion took part, the defence of Indo-China, American 'jungle green', clothing was worn in the field, with American – and later, French – steel helmets, and Australian-style bush hats. The white *képi* was worn when not in action, with pale drill bush shirts and trousers, or shorts. A dark brown battledress was issued, for parade wear in the rainy season, in the mid-1950s.

G1 Sergent, 2e Régiment Étranger Parachutiste, 1970

This N.C.O., identified by double gold chevrons on each upper arm, wears the tunic and trousers currently issued as walking-out dress, and also worn on certain occasions as 'No. 1' dress. The pentagonal lapel badges carry a gold grenade under three green chevrons, a motif repeated on the stiff midnight-blue shoulder-boards. The chevrons on these items do not have a rank connotation, and are worn by all from *légionnaire* to *colonel*. The green Legion tie was simply 'acquired' and is now an official distinction of the corps; large stocks of green ties were available in Indo-China during the late 1940s, and the Legion used them to fill their requirements without official sanction. The *képi*, midnight blue with a red top and gold false chinstrap and grenade badge, is the standard issue; on achieving the rank of *caporal-chef* the wearer discards the white cotton cover. Parachute wings in silver-finish metal are pinned above the right breast pocket, and the regimental badge hangs from the button of that pocket on a leather fob. The bright red braided shoulder-cord is peculiar to the 2e R.E.P.

G2 Légionnaire drummer, 3e Régiment Étranger d'Infanterie, 1970

This musician wears the Legion's battledress with ceremonial additions – the parade epaulettes, sash, and white belt, gloves and gaiters. The diamond-shaped arm badge is clearly visible; the drum hangings bear the colours of the Legion – red and green – and the motto 'Legio Patria Nostra' – 'The Legion is our homeland'.

G3 Caporal, 1er Régiment Étranger, 1970

A junior N.C.O. in parade dress; the battledress carries no lapel badges, in contrast to the tunic, but is the only winter uniform to which ceremonial epaulettes are added. The rank chevrons on the left arm are butted down against the standard arm badge. Note the spat-type gaiters; both this and the type depicted in G2 are currently in use by different units. The regimental badge is suspended from the breast pocket. The rifle is the F.S.A. 49/56.

H1 Légionnaire pioneer, 13e D.B.L.E., 1970

This figure depicts the traditionally bearded pioneer; a squad of pioneers, with polished axes and hide aprons, play an important part in each regiment's ceremonial, and maintain traditions which date from Napoleon's day. Crossed axes in gold are worn in a green-edged, midnight-blue diamond on the right upper arm, balancing the grenade badge on the left arm. The parade epaulettes of pioneers and colour parties have gold crescents. The green-and-gold braided cord is peculiar to this regiment, referring to the colours of the Médaille Militaire awarded for the 13e D.B.L.E.'s services in the Second World War. The tie is tucked between the buttons of the shirt in the centre of the chest, as always with Legion shirt-sleeve order. The light shirt and trousers are worn in place of battledress as summer uniform.

H2 Capitaine, 3e R.E.I., 1970

This officer wears summer-weight tunic and trousers, and is in 'No. 1' dress. The red-topped *képi* bears a gold knot design and the three gold bands around the top rim indicate rank. The three stripes of a captain are repeated across the end of the epaulette. Many officers move from regiment to regiment within the Legion, and this infantry officer wears parachutist's qualification wings on the right breast. Note the pentagonal lapel badges, and the green waistcoat visible in the throat of the tunic. The red double shoulder-cord worn by this regiment recalls the Legion d'Honneur awarded to the R.M.L.E. in the First World War.

H3 Légionnaire de première classe, 2e R.E.P., Tchad, 1970

The paratroopers of the Legion detachment currently on active service in Tchad wear a green twill combat jacket and trousers, invariably with rolled sleeves, and jump-boots. For desert operations the green beret with the paratroopers' cap badge is discarded in favour of the bush hat. Modern webbing combat equipment is worn, ammunition belts for the A.A.52 light machine-gun are carried round the waist or shoulders, and bright neck-scarves are popular. The only insignia is the diamond-shaped arm badge and the single green chevron of rank.